War
Classics

READ & REMEMBER

War Classics

The Remarkable Memoir
of Scottish Scholar
CHRISTINA KEITH
on the Western Front

EDITED BY FLORA JOHNSTON

FLORA JOHNSTON has a First Class Honours degree in Scottish History and a postgraduate qualification in Museum Studies. She worked for six years for the National Museums of Scotland on the development of their prestigious Museum of Scotland and now researches and writes historical material for publications, interpretation panels and multimedia. Her third book was published in 2012 by the Islands Book Trust, *Faith in a Crisis: Famine, Eviction and the Church in North and South Uist.*

940.48141

Cover illustrations: *Front cover:* Christina's graduation; a tank and troops at Amiens. *Back cover:* troops at Amiens.

First published 2014

The History Press
The Mill, Brimscombe Port
Stroud, Gloucestershire, GL5 2QG
www.thehistorypress.co.uk

© Christina Keith, 2014
Introductory material © Flora Johnston, 2014

The right of Christina Keith and Flora Johnston to be identified as the Authors of this work has been asserted in accordance with the Copyright, Designs and Patents Act 1988.

British Library Cataloguing in Publication Data.
A catalogue record for this book is available from the British Library.

ISBN 978 0 7509 5366 5

Typesetting and origination by The History Press
Printed in Great Britain

Contents

Acknowledgements

I would like to thank the trustees of the Kerr-Fry Bequest for the grant which allowed me time to work on Christina's manuscript and to carry out research in some of the places which were part of her story.

Archivists and librarians from the schools, universities and towns which featured in Christina's life have helped me to piece together her story, and I am grateful for help received from the following organisations: Castletown Heritage Society; Caithness Archive Centre, Wick; Edinburgh University Library; St Leonard's School, St Andrews; Newcastle University Library; Birmingham University Library; St Hilda's College, Oxford; Newnham College, Cambridge; Dieppe Ville d'Art et d'Histoire; The British School at Rome. I'm also very grateful to my agent, Robert Dudley, for his enduring faith in Christina's memoir.

The extracts from the diaries of John Wight Duff are reproduced by permission of the librarian, Robinson Library, Newcastle University.

The images from the YMCA collections are reproduced by permission of Special Collections, University of Birmingham and of the YMCA.

The letters of David Barrogill Keith are reproduced by permission of the Highland Archive Service, Caithness Archive Centre.

Particular thanks to my father, Peter Keith Morrison, for starting this whole project off by showing me Christina's memoir, for giving permission for its publication, and most of all for his many, many stories and reminiscences over the years which have fuelled my interest. I'm also grateful to his sister Joy and cousin Sheila for sharing their memories of the Keith family and of time spent in Thurso. My own family too have had to put up with my obsessions, and so thanks are due to Elizabeth and Alastair, and to David, who only once said as we pulled into another obscure French destination, 'It's like going on holiday with Christina!'

But most of all, thank you to Christina for writing all this down in the first place. I hope I have done your memoir justice.

Introduction

I never knew Christina Keith, but she was my grandmother's eldest sister. She died in 1963, just a few months after my parents became engaged. In her will she made a gift to my father, her nephew, 'to help him start off in his married life'.

In our family home there was an exceptionally long bookcase, which caused problems to the removal men each time we moved house. That bookcase had belonged to Christina Keith, or 'Auntie Tiny' as she was known within the family. She was one among a host of legendary relatives whose names I knew, an intellectual who was somewhat eccentric and took her tins to the nearby hotel to be opened because she couldn't use a tin opener.

That was largely the extent of my awareness of Auntie Tiny until November 2011, when my father first showed me her manuscript memoir from 1918 to '19. In this short book Christina, using the pseudonym 'A Fool in France', recounts her experiences as a young lecturer to the troops in France at the end of the First World War. It is a story in two parts. In the first she recalls life at the base among men who were desperate to be allowed home, while the second part describes an astonishing journey which she and a female companion took across the devastated battlefields just four months after the Armistice. From the moment I read the memoir I was captivated. I wanted to know more about Christina, her life, her background and the scheme which had taken her to France. Here was a truly fresh insight into life in France as the First World War came to a close.

I am glad that Christina wrote down her experiences. She disguised the identities of those about whom she wrote, which suggests that she always intended her story for wider circulation, and her brother appears to have tried to find a publisher for the book after her death, but without success. Yet now, a century later, Christina's story is worth telling for a number of reasons. Firstly, despite the fact that the First World War is one of the most-discussed periods in recent history, Christina describes aspects of that time which have never been particularly widely known, saying herself, 'I suppose we were one of the freak stunts of the War. You have probably never heard of us and would not have believed us true if you had.'

She travelled to France as part of the army's education scheme, which was implemented by the YMCA. Based in Dieppe, she observed at first hand the workings of the 'Lines of Communication', the immense logistical infrastructure which existed behind the front line during the four years of conflict. The fighting armies needed to be supplied with weaponry, clothing, food and equipment, which involved drivers, engineers, bakers and clerks among many others. The Remount Service supplied and cared for the horses which were still an intrinsic part of the army during this conflict. The tremendous feat of organisation involved in the Lines of Communication contributed hugely to the British Army's ability to sustain and ultimately prevail in such a prolonged conflict, yet the role played by tens of thousands of men and women behind the lines has generally been overlooked in favour of the more dramatic, glorious and tragic stories from the front line.

Christina set out for this world of base soldiers, rest camps and service huts in October 1918, just in time to participate in the newly launched education scheme. There had been educational provision for the men throughout the war, although not on the scale of this new scheme. The YMCA had played a significant role in caring for the physical, spiritual and emotional needs of the men since the outbreak of war. From officers' rest clubs in French towns to huts in army camps where female volunteers served tea and provisions to the men, from reading rooms and organised sports to the provision of accommodation near hospitals for the relatives of wounded soldiers, the YMCA's contribution to boosting morale touched men right across the army, and yet is little remembered today.[1] We are familiar with accounts of the trenches, but Christina's narrative sheds light on a parallel existence which was taking place only a few miles from the front line. Most soldiers moved between these two interdependent scenes, two parts of the same whole which made up the British soldier's experience of northern France in the First World War.

And yet Christina's story is more than simply a picture of life behind the lines. In March 1919, with four days' leave, she and a female companion (known only as 'the Hut Lady') managed to negotiate permission to travel by train into the War Zone. Her ambition was to 'see where my brothers have been and all the things they've never told me of these weary years'. This remarkable journey of two British women across a devastated landscape provides a vivid and compelling eyewitness account of a world which can only have existed in that form for a very short time.

The names of the places they visited – Arras, Vimy Ridge, Thiepval, Cambrai – are today still synonymous with slaughter. French refugees were living in abandoned army dugouts. Tanks, clothing and weaponry lay littered across the battlefield. The war graves were not grassy fields with neat white lines of stones, but groups of rough wooden crosses stuck in yellow mud and water. The sense is of a land which, now that the guns had fallen silent, was stunned by what had happened to it.

Few women had reached these parts, a fact emphasised by the surprise and delight with which Christina and her friend were met by soldiers at every turn. They knew they were privileged to pass through the army zone before much of the debris had been cleaned up – 'while it is like this and before the tourists come', said the Hut Lady. Christina described those four days as 'a dream-world, where everything happened after the heart's desire on a background of infinite horror'.

Christina's manuscript thus draws our attention to people, places and events which are half-forgotten, but what is even more remarkable is the perspective from which this narrative is written. There are many first-hand accounts of different facets of the First World War – the rise of general literacy levels ensured that this conflict was documented on a personal level to an extent that had never happened before. However the majority of diaries, letters and memoirs are, naturally, by men. There are several vivid accounts by nurses working in clearing stations and base hospitals, but Christina was a very different woman to these – and would probably have made a terrible nurse! Christina was an intellectual, a high-flying academic from a generation which was breaking down barriers in women's education. She had spent most of her adult life in the cloistered, middle-class environment of academia, living in all-female residences, and was accustomed to teaching university-level students. In 1918 she found herself in the male-dominated world of the army, meeting, working with and teaching men of all abilities and all classes, with a keen eye to observe all that went on around her. Hers is a truly fresh perspective on the events of the period.

Christina's perspective and her frankness give us an insight into the attitudes held by those of her background at that time, and some of those attitudes can surprise us and even make us feel rather uncomfortable today. Christina came from a class and a generation which were still strongly tied to the Victorian values of the era into which she had been born. Thus, although she was a woman who clearly had no intention of letting her gender limit her academic potential, she was not a feminist as we might see it today. She took a pride in not conforming to what might be expected of a woman, referring to herself as 'a bluestocking who had never cooked a dinner in her life', yet she still expected men to treat her in a particular way, and was offended when they did not – as for example with the American soldiers who did not move their belongings to make more space for her on the train. She was perfectly willing to adopt the persona of a helpless female if she felt it would help her get her way.

Early twentieth-century society was very clearly divided along class lines, and perhaps nowhere was that emphasised more explicitly than in the army, with the division between officers and other ranks. Throughout her narrative Christina wrote with warmth and respect about the ordinary British soldier, and there is no doubting the admiration she had for the men she met – but equally there is no missing the paternalistic tone, and the breadth of the chasm which existed between her own world and the lower classes. At a time when the Russian Revolution was frighteningly recent and the military powers were constantly watchful for signs of mutiny in the ranks, those in authority were expected to reinforce social hierarchies, and Christina's colleague who dared to give secret lectures on socialism was quickly removed.

Christina's narrative reveals much about prevailing attitudes to gender, to class and also to race. With regard to her own nationality Christina was a passionate Scot, missing no opportunity to identify with other Scots and to praise her own people and traditions. Perhaps influenced by Sir Walter Scott, of whom she would later write a biography, the more tartan and Highland the better! And yet in an apparent contradiction she frequently referred to herself as an Englishwoman. It seems that in the days before nationalism had become a significant political force in Scotland, Christina was using 'English' interchangeably with 'British'. And there was absolutely no doubt in her mind that the British were the greatest race on earth.

In the immediate aftermath of the war it is perhaps not surprising that her attitude to Germany was scornful and even offensive. Once again this reflects the widely held mood of the nation, reinforced by the press. What is perhaps more surprising is that this scorn was not merely reserved for the enemy but also for Britain's allies. The Germans are referred to throughout as 'the Boche', the Chinese labourers as 'Chinks'. The French are careless and cruel to animals, the Portuguese are 'the worst-behaved of all the Allies', and the Americans are dismissed as selfish and unreliable. Only the Australians and the Canadians – notably both loyal members of the British Empire – seem worthy of her respect. British imperialistic superiority was alive and well. As she came up alongside men and women of different social backgrounds and from different nationalities, Christina was candid in her opinions and thus reveals to us much about attitudes which were commonplace in the early twentieth century.

But alongside all the interesting historical information we can glean from her writing, Christina's narrative is worthy of a wide readership because of the simple humanity of her story. Here is a woman who lived through the war, whose brothers served in the fighting and who lost people dear to her, but who says little of her own experiences. Yet despite the sorrow and tragedy which exist as a quiet undertone, here too is a woman eager to grasp the opportunities which this war gave to her. And therein lies the contradiction, for Christina as for many others. In the midst of conflict there was opportunity. In the midst of horror there was comradeship. The cost of this war was unprecedented and appalling, but there were those for whom it opened doors – to new places, to new friendships, to new skills, or simply to a new way of looking at the world.

For Christina Keith, these six months in Dieppe were a window of freedom in a life restricted by the boundaries of convention. She revelled in meeting new people, encountering new viewpoints, welcoming a wealth of new experiences and even in having her preconceptions challenged. The enchantment of it all lay as much in the fact that she and those around her knew that this world they inhabited was a fleeting one, that they would be required to return to the restrictions and realities of British routine. They could not yet know that the magnitude of what they had lived through meant that British society would never again be the same.

Notes

1. For a detailed study of the role of the YMCA in the First World War, see Michael Snape's *The Back Parts of War*, 2009.

Part 1

Christina's Story

'Living with the ancestors'

•

'An Edinburgh and Newnham girl'

•

'How fine their sense of duty has been'

•

'The meeting of mind with mind'

1

'Living with the ancestors'

Christina Keith was born on 12 January 1889 in the little town of Thurso on the furthest north coast of Scotland. It was noon, so even on those short, dark winter days some light would have spilled in through the windows of the two-storey terraced house at 5 Princes Street as she entered the world. She was the first child of solicitor Peter Keith and his young wife Katie Bruce, born into a family which had deep roots in the Caithness countryside and a remarkable desire to reach beyond the ordinary.

Christina loved Caithness, that unique landscape with its huge skies and grey seas, where the light and the weather reflect the extremes of living on the very northern edge of mainland Scotland. She travelled far throughout her life for education, for work and for adventure, but Caithness drew her back in her retirement, and she ended her days as a writer living in the house in which she had been born. The decades in between had seen the Keith family prosper, expand and scatter, but Peter and Katie's various homes in and around Thurso provided a focal point to which their children and grandchildren continued to return.

For this was the ancestral land. Peter's family for generations back had lived in Castletown, a village in the parish of Olrig a few miles to the east of Thurso. He was born in 1847, the son of a tailor and the second-youngest child in a large family. Peter began his education at the local school, but this came to an abrupt halt when he was expelled for locking the dominie in the school building. He was then sent to the school of Matthew Dunnet in the nearby village of Bower. Matthew Dunnet had gained a significant reputation for education and boys were sent to him from far afield.[1] Peter clearly flourished under Matthew Dunnet's tuition, and perhaps it was partly under the schoolmaster's influence that he came to place such a high value on education, a value which he would pass on to Christina and his other children.

After serving a three-year apprenticeship with a Thurso solicitor, Peter travelled in 1867 to Edinburgh where he continued his training with a legal firm and also studied at the university. During this time the 1871 census reveals him lodging in Bellevue, Edinburgh, with a Caithness family. Also living there was his 21-year-old sister Johanna, the youngest member of the Keith family, who was described as a student. We do not know what Johanna was studying, or where, but this is the earliest indication of a desire for higher education among the women of the Keith family. In 1871 Edinburgh University was still an all-male enclave, but a fierce campaign was being fought for the rights of women to a higher education, led by Sophia Jex-Blake who wished to study medicine. Since 1868 the Edinburgh Ladies' Education Association had offered university-level lectures to women, with the stated aim not of training them for professions but of improving their minds. Johanna's name does not appear in the Association's class registers, which rather suggest rooms full of Edinburgh ladies from wealthy New Town addresses. Although we do not know where Johanna was studying, it is interesting to note that Christina's aunt was there as a student in Edinburgh in the very earliest days of the struggle for higher education for women.[2]

Education was valued not just on Christina's father's side but also on her mother's. Katie Bruce was without doubt a very intelligent woman. My father remembers that he and his family were in Thurso on holiday at the outbreak of the Second World War. In the uncertainty of those early months they decided to stay on in Caithness rather than return to Edinburgh. Katie took on the education of her young grandson, and when sometime later he did return to his school in Edinburgh, he was far ahead of his fellow pupils!

At the age of forty Peter Keith, now a successful solicitor, bank agent and factor to the local landlord, apparently decided it was time to get married. The story goes that he was considering one local girl and took someone into his confidence. This friend is said to have asked him if he hadn't considered Katie Bruce – she might not have the material advantages that the other girl had, but she was a very clever young woman. Peter took the advice, and they were married in April 1888.

But what was Katie's own story? Like her husband she was of Caithness heritage. On her mother's side she was descended from a family of some wealth and local influence – her grandfather lived in Freswick House and farmed 200 acres. But Katie's own childhood was not an easy one. In 1875, when she was just eleven, her father died of pneumonia, leaving her mother a widow with two children. William Bruce, whose origins were humbler than his wife's, was a wine merchant who had expanded at some point before his death into keeping a hotel. In the 1881 census his widow was continuing to run the hotel, and her 15-year-old son was working in the bank. It might have been expected that 17-year-old Katie would be helping her mother in the hotel – but no. In another of those signposts which point forward towards the role education would play in the next generation of this family, Katie Bruce was not in Caithness at all, but was living more than 250 miles away in Great King Street, Edinburgh, enrolled in 'Miss Balmain's Establishment for the Board and Education of Young Ladies'.

At this time there were many girls' schools in Edinburgh offering an education to the daughters of the middle classes. Some were larger institutions but many, like Miss Balmain's school, were substantial private houses which took a small number of boarders and perhaps some day pupils. While their brothers were being prepared for university in academies and grammar schools, the emphasis in most girls' schools was on languages, music and dancing. Visiting masters offered tuition in some subjects, while others were the domain of the resident female staff. In 1881 Jemima Balmain ran her school along with three other female teachers, one of whom was German. They had eight resident pupils, and four servants. Miss Balmain advertised her school in the following terms:

> The number of Young Ladies received as Boarders being very limited, the most careful attention is paid to each in regard to health, moral and religious training, the preparation of their various studies, and their comfort in every respect. The First Masters attend to give instruction in all the branches of a thorough education and accomplishments, and Miss Balmain is assisted by Foreign and English Governesses. French and German conversation daily. [3]

So despite difficult circumstances at home, by the age of 17 and probably earlier, Katie was living in Edinburgh in order to receive 'a thorough education and accomplishments', in a move which surely influenced the approach she and Peter would take to the education of their own children a generation later.

In 1888 at the age of 24, Katie married Peter Keith. The bride, the groom and their wider families all lived in or around Thurso … and yet the wedding took place far away in St John's church, Southall, in London. Some members of the family made the long journey down to London, for two of the witnesses were Katie's younger brother John, and William Keith, Peter's oldest brother. Peter gave his place of residence as Thurso, but Katie said she was living in Southall. We cannot be sure what she was doing there, but the third witness at the wedding was a young woman of Katie's own age called Mary Etherington. Mary was a teacher of music at a girls' school in Southall which her mother, also Mary, ran. Perhaps Katie was also teaching at the school? By the time of her marriage at the age of 24, Katie Bruce had lived in both Edinburgh and London, and she would pass those wider horizons on to her own children.

After a honeymoon in Paris, Peter and Katie returned to Thurso, and Christina was born the following year. They soon moved into the Bank House, a large home built above the premises of the British Linen Bank. This was where they lived in the winter months, but they spent their summers in 'The Cottage', above the shore beside Thurso Castle, where Peter Keith was factor to Sir John Tollemache Sinclair.

In 1913 Peter Keith purchased Olrig House, which was the 'big house' in the parish in which he had grown up, but by this time Christina was living away from Thurso. Many years later, writing to her mother, Christina said, 'I love the Cottage – it is quite the nicest house we have.' She was conscious of the influence her childhood surroundings had had on her. She remembered how her father, who had been factor to the owners of Barrogill Castle (now the Castle of Mey) for many years, had stepped in when the castle and its contents were to be sold, and had purchased portraits of the 14th Earl of Caithness and his first wife, the Countess Louise, after whom he and Katie had named their second daughter. These portraits hung on the walls in the Bank House:

> So the portraits moved to another home, to be landmarks for other children, who found, to their surprise, a subtle atmosphere of gaiety and splendour and high distinction somehow wafted from their presence. Living with 'the ancestors' had nothing everyday about it. They swept you up into their own lively world.[4]

The family grew. When Christina was two, her little brother David Barrogill, known in the family as Barr, was born, followed the next year by Catherine Louise. Barrogill and Louise would both follow their father into law and would practice in Thurso. Barrogill later became Sheriff Substitute in Kirkwall, but his first love was art, and while training to be a lawyer he also studied painting at the Académie de l'Écluse in Paris and drawing at Edinburgh College of Art. Barrogill too had absorbed the family passion for an education which was genuinely stimulating. Writing for his school's former pupils' magazine (which he helped to found), he observed:

> Education has become too lop-sided – so much attention is given to memorising, so little to thinking. This cannot but adversely affect individuality. Burns would never have been Burns if he had been a slavish imitator of Shakespeare.[5]

In qualifying and practising as a lawyer in the 1920s Louise, like her older sister, took her place in a world which had very recently belonged exclusively to men. The *John o' Groats Journal* from December 1928 illustrates Louise's achievement perfectly. A photograph of the Caithness Society of Solicitors, taken at Olrig House during a garden party, shows Louise surrounded by thirteen male colleagues including her father Peter and her brother Barrogill. The photographer has positioned her in the centre of the group, his eye drawn perhaps to the dramatic contrast created between her simple, light-coloured blouse and hat, and the dark suits of the men. It is a desperate tragedy that Louise, the lightness amid the sobriety in that image, would die within a year of the photograph being taken.

Peter and Katie's next two children were both daughters, Julia and Mildred. They too studied at Edinburgh University and both worked in Paris as typists at the peace conference at the conclusion of the First World War, living in the Grand Hotel Majestic. They regularly saw the leading political figures of the day, including Lloyd George, Churchill and Marshal Foch, at dinner, and witnessed first hand many momentous events such as the victory parade through Paris in 1919. When Christina hoped to visit 'my sister in Paris' from Dieppe, it was Julia and Mildred she had in mind. Julia later returned to Thurso, but Mildred's long career would take her to cities including Warsaw, Prague and Buenos Aires. She wrote each week to her mother, and those letters today offer a fascinating chronicle of Foreign Office diplomatic society between the wars.

Of the four youngest children, William had a successful career in the navy, and my grandmother Patricia shared Barrogill's passion for painting, studying at art college. Archibald died as an infant in 1904. Edward, the youngest, was born in 1908, and thus was nearly twenty years younger than Christina. He too followed a successful legal career.

Scattered as they were, Katie wrote to each of her children every week and kept many of the letters they sent in reply. There were the burdens, strains and disagreements of life in a large family. There is no doubt Peter and Katie put a great deal of pressure on their children to succeed academically, and that pressure perhaps suited some of them more than others. All the children were encouraged to achieve, but it was Christina, the eldest, whom the family believed to be truly exceptional. In the daily routine of family life this led to some irritation, as she was exempted from chores which the others were expected to perform, but above all they were proud of her. Christina, the eldest, was the pioneer.

Notes

1. Henrietta Munro, 'A Caithness School in the Early Nineteenth Century', *Caithness Field Club Bulletin*, 1981
2. Records of the Edinburgh Ladies' Education Association, Edinburgh University Archives
3. Edinburgh and Leith Post Office Directory 1880–81
4. Christina Keith, *The Romance of Barrogill Castle*
5. Allan Lannon, *Miller Academy History and Memories for the Millennium*

2

'An Edinburgh and Newnham girl'

Christina was born in 1889, the year of the Universities (Scotland) Act which would pave the way for the admission of women to Scottish universities from 1892. Thus, by the time she started school as a little girl in Thurso, a door had recently been opened through which she would gladly walk some years later.

Things were changing, but slowly. The traditional curriculum which educated girls for their assumed domestic role, be that as servants, as wives and mothers, or as ladies of leisure, persisted for a long time, excluding girls from entering university by denying them the required classical subjects. The financial commitment involved in supporting daughters towards and through university – particularly when many bursaries were only open to boys – also deterred some parents from encouraging their daughters into higher education. For although various professions now admitted single women, they remained firmly closed to married women. Why pay to educate a daughter who would not be able to pursue a career once she had married?

Christina was privileged to have supportive parents who encouraged her in her education and who had the financial resources to help her. Without these two factors it would have been hard if not impossible for her to achieve what she did. Many intelligent women of her generation were unable to pursue their dreams – equality was a long way off. But Peter and Katie not only approved of education, they actively encouraged it. One obituary to Peter Keith on his death in 1936 emphasised his passion for learning:

> His chief outside interest may, however, be said to have been education, and for many years he was a leading member of the Thurso School Board, helping not a little to raise the prestige of higher education in the north of Scotland. … He had a firm belief in the value of education and his own family consisting of three sons and five daughters lived up to his belief.[1]

Christina began her schooling at the Miller Institute in Thurso, and her potential was quickly apparent. In 1903, aged 14, she was dux of the school, and it was around this time that her parents decided to send her south to continue her education, presumably with a view to qualifying her for university. She was sent firstly to St Leonard's School in St Andrews, which opened in 1877 as the first girls' school in Scotland run along English public school lines, and which offered a full curriculum. This was Christina's first experience of living in an all-female institution, the type of environment in which she would spend much of her life, but she was unhappy. We cannot be sure why, but she may well have disliked the games which were an important part of school life at St Leonard's – 'I never am any good at running,' she observed, after sprinting to catch the train in Amiens.

Christina left St Leonard's and moved to a school in Edinburgh which had echoes of Miss Balmain's establishment, her mother's former school. Miss Williamson ran a boarding and day school in Abercromby Place, just a few streets away from the property which had housed Miss Balmain's school. But a generation had passed since Katie came to school in Edinburgh, and those decades had been significant ones for women's education. Miss Williamson's school emphasised the opportunities available for women at university, offering 'university-trained mistresses' as well as visiting masters, and stating that pupils would be prepared for the required exams for Edinburgh University and for Girton and Newnham Colleges in Cambridge.[2]

The Keiths must have been satisfied with Miss Williamson's school, which later became St Serf's, for some of their younger daughters were also sent there. Christina sat the necessary preliminary examinations and entered Edinburgh University. She had by this time learned Latin, and announced her intention of studying for Honours in classics – despite not yet even knowing the Greek alphabet. So during her first year at university, alongside her other classes she learned the basics of Greek, and in her second year picked it up at university level, taking the class medal at the end of the year. The professor of Greek at the time was A.W. Mair, who was described by Christina's brother Barrogill as 'the brightest, dearest and most twinkling in all that glorious firmament'.[3]

During her time at the university, Christina lived in Masson Hall, the women's hostel in George Square which had opened in 1897. It was named after David Masson, professor of rhetoric and English language, who had been an influential supporter of the campaign for women's higher education and had provided lectures in English literature to the Edinburgh Ladies' Education Association. The warden of the hostel was Frances Simson, who was herself one of the very first women to graduate from Edinburgh University and who was involved in an unsuccessful campaign all the way to the House of Lords to obtain the right for women graduates to vote for the University MP. Masson Hall not only provided accommodation for those women students who, like Christina, had come from further afield, it also offered a place of communal focus for all women students, who were able to meet there and use the facilities.

In 1920 Peter Keith had cause to write to *The Scotsman* about a dispute which was taking place within Masson Hall after the retirement of Frances Simson, and he expressed his satisfaction with the living arrangements of his daughters at Edinburgh University:

As the parent of one of the 33 young ladies presently in residence in Masson Hall, I am personally interested in the matter. Other members of my family have been in residence in that Hall for the last twelve years, almost without a break. It is gratifying to be able to say that, without exception during all that long period, while the late Warden was in charge, the young ladies in the Hall were most comfortable and happy. The discipline during her time was perfect, and there was never any trouble. Of course, in an institution of the kind it is absolutely essential that there must be proper discipline.[4]

That 'proper discipline' would have included strict regulations about meeting with men, particularly in private spaces. A way of life bound by regulations and conventions was one to which Christina would become accustomed and, as a tutor to young female students, one in which she later no doubt participated as a chaperone and figure of authority. It was in part the freedom from this 'discipline' which she found so exhilarating in Dieppe.

On 31 March 1910, Christina crossed the floor of the McEwan Hall, a small, slight figure, and was 'capped'. Peter and Katie were probably watching among the assembled relatives and friends as their eldest daughter graduated with

First Class Honours in Latin, Greek and classical archaeology – subjects which so recently had been considered a waste of time for a girl to learn. Of the ten others in her class graduating that day, nine were men. For her parents this was surely not only a moment of immense pride but the fruit of their own commitment to education which had reached back to the days when the doors of the university were firmly closed to women.

But for Christina this first degree was not the culmination of her education, but a stepping stone to further study. She had decided by this time to pursue a career in classical scholarship and academia, which was still a highly unusual path for a young woman to take. It is probably significant that at this point Christina took steps to continue her studies under the guidance of the two pioneering women in her chosen field, Eugénie Strong and Jane Ellen Harrison.

Along with another Edinburgh student Christina was awarded the Rhind Classical Scholarship, which was worth about £85 a year for two years. Before her graduation in March she also travelled down to Newnham College, Cambridge, and sat the exam for a separate Classical scholarship. She was successful, and was awarded an additional £50 a year for three years.[5]

Having secured this funding, Christina was set to return to Newnham in the autumn, but she had an adventure to undertake first. She left Edinburgh soon after her graduation, and early in April she arrived in Rome, where she would spend the next few months studying at the British School at Rome. This research institute had only recently been established, in 1901. Its assistant director was Eugénie Strong, an archaeologist and leading scholar of Roman art. The school's *Annual Report* for 1910 records Christina's time in Rome:

> Miss Christina Keith, MA, University of Edinburgh, reached Rome early in April, and devoted herself to the study of sculpture. Towards the end of her time she began under Mrs Strong's direction to specialise in Archaic Greek Sculpture. Miss Keith has recently gone to Newnham College, Cambridge, with a scholarship, but it is hoped that this promising young student may return to the School to resume her archaeological studies.

It seems Rome was just an interlude, an opportunity for twenty-one-year-old Christina to spend time living abroad and to develop her research interests. It speaks of her spirit of adventure and her readiness to welcome new experiences, an eagerness which would carry her to France and the army just eight years later, when the pleasant landscapes of Europe had become a vast field of death, grief and pain.

From Rome in October 1910 she returned to England and to Cambridge, where she would spend the next three years as a college scholar at Newnham. She excelled academically, just as she had done at Edinburgh, and was placed in the First Class in both parts of the Classical Tripos (Cambridge Honours examination). But there was one significant difference with Edinburgh. Neither Cambridge nor Oxford were yet prepared to award degrees to women. Christina was allowed to sit the exams, and was awarded a grade, but received at the time no formal qualification for her years of study at Cambridge. The awarding of degrees to women was fiercely and aggressively resisted, and was a topic of controversy during the time Christina was a student in Cambridge. The letter pages of *The Times* include many examples of strongly held opinions on both sides of the argument, including this letter from May 1913, written just as Christina was completing her Classical Tripos examinations to a level which would surpass many of her male contemporaries:

> If the ladies of Girton, Newnham, Somerville and the rest of them want to stand on an equal footing with men, why on earth don't they cut the painter with Oxford, Cambridge &c., link their colleges into an All-England Female University, and issue their own female degrees? The kind of parasitic prestige they are out for at present involves a humiliating confession of sexual inferiority.[6]

The unequal status of men and women at Cambridge created an atmosphere very different from the one Christina had known in Edinburgh. Because the battle was still to be won, female students knew that any apparent failure on their part, be it academic or moral, could damage their cause.[7] Strict regulations governed the conduct of female students. Chaperones were often required to accompany them to lectures. Walking in the street with a man was forbidden – which was sometimes awkward when moving together from one class to another. A woman could only entertain a brother or a father in her room, and in those circumstances her friends would not be allowed to be present. Propriety was everything.

There is no suggestion that Christina was inclined to rebel against these rules; rather, it was because she was so accustomed to a life in which the rules of respectability were understood by all that her six months in France involved such a sense of transformation. A natural and gifted student, she relished all that Cambridge had to offer her academically without, at that time, apparently being frustrated by its conventions. One outstanding figure from whom Christina could learn was another pioneering academic, Jane Harrison. Like Eugénie Strong, Jane Harrison's unconventional life demonstrated to her students that it might be difficult to be a successful female classical scholar but it was not impossible.

Jane Harrison had held a research fellowship at Newnham since 1898. She taught students in Part II of the Classical Tripos who were specialising in her own research interests of art and archaeology. She almost certainly taught Christina. She was an unconventional and inspirational teacher, whose methods were perhaps best suited to the most gifted students. Her second significant publication on Greek religion was published during Christina's time at Newnham, and her work has since been highly influential. At a time when academic women were under great scrutiny Harrison became a controversial figure, and was criticised not only because of her feminist approach to her work but also as a pacifist and an atheist. Harrison formed a very close friendship with a student, Hope Mirrlees, who would have been well known to Christina as they arrived at Newnham in the same year, although Hope never completed the Tripos.[8]

Christina left Newnham, and took the next step in her own career as a professional female academic by applying for the vacant post of lecturer in classics at Armstrong College, Newcastle, which was part of the University of Durham. She and four other candidates were interviewed on 16 June 1914 by Professor John Wight Duff, who recorded in his diary, 'My new assistant to succeed my "second-in-command" is an Edinburgh and Newnham girl.'[9]

Professor Duff spent some time that day explaining to her what her duties would be when she took up her position in October. Perhaps he showed her round the college itself with its grand buildings, parts of which were newly completed, and took her into the college library. A few months later, Christina believed, she would be walking these corridors and lecturing in these halls.

But Christina would never teach in the buildings she saw that day, and would never use the college library. By the time she returned to take up her post in October 1914, war had broken out and everything had changed.

Notes

1. *The Scotsman*, 19 December 1936
2. Advertisements in various editions of *The Scotsman*, 1903–08
3. David Barrogill Keith, 'Bygone Days at Edinburgh University' in *University of Edinburgh Journal*, spring 1965

4. *The Scotsman,* 30 June 1920
5. *The Scotsman,* 1 April 1910; *The Times,* 6 August 1910
6. *The Times,* 23 May 1913
7. See, for example, anecdotes in (ed.) Ann Philips, *A Newnham Anthology,* 1979
8. Annabel Robinson, *The Life and Work of Jane Ellen Harrison,* 2002, and Hugh Lloyd-Jones, 'Jane Ellen Harrison', in *Oxford Dictionary of National Biography*
9. Diaries of John Wight Duff in Newcastle University Archives

3

'How fine their sense
of duty has been'

In October 1914, when Christina came to Newcastle to take up her first
post as a lecturer, her brother Barrogill had already enlisted in the army
and was at a training camp in Nigg in the north of Scotland. Young men
from Armstrong College whom she would have otherwise taught had similarly
left their studies to become part of the British Expeditionary Force. The college buildings had been requisitioned and turned into a military hospital, and
would not be returned to the university until the war was over, by which time
Christina had moved on.

Professor Duff returned from his summer holiday and spent a busy few weeks
putting arrangements in place to allow his courses to continue in these drasti-
cally altered circumstances. He arranged for students to use the public library,
and for lectures to take place in the Literary and Philosophical Society building
in the town. Books, chairs and blackboards needed to be transported to the
new venue. Every time he wanted access to his own college rooms to remove
papers or to the college library he had to apply for a special permit. Duff's
diaries clearly reveal how irritating he found this set of circumstances, but he
also recognised his inconvenience was inconsequential when compared with
the tragedy just beginning to unfold in the trenches of the Western Front. A few
weeks after term had begun, Duff took Christina with him into the old college:

I took Miss Keith, my lecturer, to Armstrong College or as it is now 'The Northern General Hospital'. We spoke to several men wounded as recently as last Friday near Armentiers and round Lille in the stubborn fighting against the Germans – 'Scots Greys', Irish cavalrymen and Northumberland Fusiliers.

One of the men to whom they spoke that day told them that 'three of his friends had been shot close to him, and much that he had seen he could not forget'.[1]

Christina's first experiences as a lecturer were dominated by the war. Each week more and more young men left for the front, and over the months word came back of students and former students who had been injured or killed. Those who did not leave were the subject of suspicion and even scorn, such as Christina's fellow lecturer in the classics department who tried and failed to gain military exemption:

One of my former Honours students appeared in the khaki of a second lieutenant to say goodbye before leaving for four months' training. Every other week men like him look in to see me, and tell me of their whereabouts. How fine their sense of duty has been: so the old nation is not decadent – except for logic-chopping objectors like my miserable lecturer.[2]

All those young men Christina had known, from Thurso, from Edinburgh, from Cambridge and now from Newcastle, all of an age to fight in this terrible war and many of them never to return. Of her own brothers, Barrogill was fighting in the trenches with the 12th Scottish Rifles and Willie was in service with the navy, seeing action at the Battle of Jutland. Little Edward was still a child at home in Caithness. The war dominated their world, and yet in other ways ordinary university life continued. At the end of Christina's first term the staff of the classics department met to mark exams and work out class lists. Duff noted in his diary that they continued late into the night 'to enable Miss Keith to leave at 1.31 in the morning for her home in Thurso – a journey north of 15 hours'. She left him with a Christmas present of a brace of grouse, presumably sent down from Caithness.[3]

In March 1916 Christina read a paper on 'People one would have liked to meet at Rome' to the Northumberland and Durham Classical Association, a paper which Duff described as 'a tastefully conceived and composed effort of historical imagination'.[4] Although overshadowed by war, her years in Newcastle appear to have passed successfully. By May 1918 she had applied for and been accepted as classics tutor in St Hilda's College, Oxford – a return to the female collegiate life she had known in Cambridge. She was now twenty-nine years old. But at this point her career as a lecturer took an unexpected and dramatic turn. In July 1918, Sir Henry Hadow, Principal of Armstrong College, was appointed Director of Education for the Forces in France. Whether he made a direct approach to Christina, or whether she merely heard about the scheme and in typical style decided this was something of which she wanted to be part, she changed her plans. St Hilda's agreed that she could delay her arrival in Oxford in order to take up a position as staff lecturer with the troops in France.

Christina was off to Dieppe.

Notes

1. John Wight Duff diaries, 28 October 1914
2. John Wight Duff diaries, 3 March 1916
3. John Wight Duff diaries, December 1914
4. John Wight Duff diaries, 4 March 1916

4

'The meeting of
mind with mind'

In the summer of 1918 the War Office appointed the YMCA as agent to put in place a systematic scheme of voluntary education for the troops in France. The YMCA had already demonstrated its commitment and ability to provide education alongside other aspects of its work with the army, and the backing of the War Office enabled the establishment of a more comprehensive scheme than had been possible before. The best educationalists and lecturers were to be put at the disposal of the army.

As Director of Education, Sir Henry Hadow recruited a series of sub-directors who would implement the scheme in different geographical areas. Christina was based in Dieppe, working under sub-director Henry Brooke, whom she refers to as 'the Chief', and travelling out to huts and camps across the area. As well as having its own local base, 'the School', Dieppe was the location for the headquarters of the whole scheme and for the central library of books – probably a good place to be based. The papers of Albert Percy Braddock, sub-director at Abbeville, give an insight into the day-to-day running of the scheme. They mirror much of Christina's account, but also reveal frustration with the logistical problems of setting up such a scheme – lack of staff, lack of equipment and books, and lack of transport.[1]

Sir Henry's first few months were so successful that in October he was transferred to become an adviser on education at the War Office, and Sir Graham Balfour was appointed as the new director. Graham Balfour, cousin and biographer of Robert Louis Stevenson, was Director of Education for Staffordshire. Some months into her time in Dieppe Christina was given a role organising correspondence classes, and was given an office in General Headquarters, based in the Hotel des Étrangers on the seafront – in which, ironically, Robert Louis Stevenson had stayed. She noted, 'I was installed in a beautiful big room on the first floor, directly opposite the Education Chief himself.' This was Sir Graham Balfour.

Of course, when the YMCA and the War Office worked together to set up this scheme in the summer of 1918, they could not know that the Armistice would be signed in November. This did not bring an end to the scheme, but it brought a significant change to the type of work that Christina and her colleagues had imagined they would undertake. Sir Graham Balfour wrote, 'Owing to the unexpected developments of the War, to the sudden Armistice and the accelerated Demobilisation, the whole scope and nature of this Education was different from what both administrators and teachers had been led to expect.'[2]

Many of the men recognised the wisdom of taking advantage of an offer of free training, be it vocational or academic, before returning to rebuild their lives in Britain after the war. As one writer in the YMCA magazine *The Red Triangle* noted, some young men had 'not only risked their lives in the great cause, but sacrificed educational opportunities which are not likely to fall to them again'.[3] In September, 234 men attended lectures in the Dieppe and Le Tréport area. By November, when Christina's work was in full swing, this stood at 813. The classes reached their maximum in December, with 2,296 attending, then began to fall away as men were demobilised, returning to 661 in February.[4]

In the spring of 1919, the War Office decided to take over the organisation of education in the army, and the YMCA scheme was wound up. It was a programme of education which, although it lasted for only a short time, impacted the lives of many men and influenced the future educational structure within the army. It was described as 'the largest system of adult education which has ever at one time been launched from this country'.[5] Ideas about education were at the forefront of wider discussions as Britain looked towards creating a new peacetime society. The founding principle on which Peter and Katie had raised their children in distant Caithness – the value of true education – was spreading out to reach male and female, rich and poor, with consequences far beyond any they might themselves have imagined:

The war has done such a lot for education; it has forced us to think about things … Once you get people really thinking and discussing together the results of their thinking, there is no knowing what may happen. It is the meeting of mind with mind which really changes the face of the world.[6]

Notes

1. Papers of Albert Percy Braddock in the University of Birmingham Special Collections
2. Letter from Graham Balfour among the Papers of Albert Percy Braddock
3. *The Red Triangle*, August 1918
4. *A Short Record of the Education Work of the YMCA with the British Armies in France*
5. *Ibid.*
6. *The Red Triangle*, June 1918

Part 2

~<small>ՊՊ</small>~

Christina Keith's Memoir

A Fool in France

To the nicest of all the pippins
Who sleeps near La Bassée.

Author's Preface to the Reader.

I have been asked whether this book is true. To maintain that it is so is not, as Socrates said once long ago, worthy of a wise man. It would take a fool, as you will agree, to write it. And for its truth? I can only remind you of what Bismarck did, when he wished not to be believed. He always told the truth.

Christina Keith

Our little hour, – how swift it flies
When poppies flare and lilies smile;
How soon the fleeting minute dies,
Leaving us but a little while
To dream our dream, to sing our song,
To pick the fruit, to pluck the flower.
The Gods – They do not give us long, –
One little hour.

(by Leslie Coulson, 1889–8 October 1916, in From an outpost and other poems,
published in 1917 by his father)

1

How I went out

Of all the sideshows run by the British Army in the field, the most entertaining – as it is in general the least known – was surely its system of education. Lest 'entertaining' be misunderstood, I hasten to add that the War Office itself places education under the head of Amusements. Much has been heard – and deservedly – of the canteens that fed the men and gave them games and cinemas, of the concert parties and dramatic parties that performed at every base and at most of the camps behind the lines, but early in 1918 there came a glut of all these. The men were not satisfied with being merely fed and amused. And then there dawned the 'preposterous' idea of education. Why should the men not be taught something when they came weary out of the trenches, or when they lay at rest camps, or in their leisure hours at the Bases? No idea could seem more ridiculous at first sight than that Thomas Atkins and his officers should go back to school again in the intervals of their fighting. But go back again they did – many of them at least – and thoroughly enjoyed the experience.

So curiously interwoven are mind and body that for intense physical strain the only true reaction is a mental one. If the balance of mind and body is to be preserved, the mind too must work. Mere amusement does not grip the mind sufficiently to provide a counter-balancing strain.

Not that the soldier or his officer ever argued the point. The keynote of the Army Education System in France was its voluntariness. And a second point was that the great majority of the staff who carried out the education were women. Some might question how a woman – other than a nurse – could be attached to an army and still remain respectable. Yet while it lasted, it was both a respectable and a thrilling life. These brief notes will endeavour to show how it was both.

It was summer 1918 before we began. I suppose we were one of the freak stunts of the War. You have probably never heard of us and would not have believed us true if you had.

'No doubt you will be giving us Latin exercises to do in the trenches,' said the Army brother bitterly, on the news of my appointment, 'and improving our grammar by the way.'[1]

'I haven't been told yet what my duties will be,' I rejoined cautiously.

'Sort of Hush Hush Department, eh?' he growled sarcastically.

That and an intense mystification on the part of those who had been there, were the usual results of the information that I was being sent to France. 'Whatever for?' I was asked more than once, with somewhat discomfiting bluntness. I took refuge in the statement of the Authorities. 'They call me,' I quoted, 'Staff Lecturer on Education on the Lines of Communication.'

'My Hat!' – 'Eyewash!' – 'You don't say so!' – 'They do think of everything, don't they?' – were some of the many irreverent comments this drew forth. As we lived in the neighbourhood of a big Naval station, I was exhibited triumphantly to passing Naval officers by the SNO's wife [Senior Naval Officer] as the latest freak that was going to France.[2] Over their teacups they looked at me with silent bewilderment. I flatter myself that I provided an interesting topic of conversation in the gunroom of more than one battleship in August 1918. 'Would the Navy be the next to be educated?' was the dismaying thought in most minds, but it was usually dismissed with scorn. Who would want an educated Navy?

September came and I was still at home – not one step nearer France. Voluminous correspondence, even occasional telegrams passed between London and myself. They wanted to know if I had received their previous letter – if not, this was what it said. Was I quite content to be Staff Lecturer? Did I like my salary? Would I prefer it to be more or less? Please get the uniform at once.

Myself – to London, by return. Had received and replied to their former letter. Was quite content with salary, title, etc. What was the uniform and when did they want me?

London – to me. Yes the salary was quite nice but on the whole they thought they would halve it. Please get the uniform at once – underlined.

Myself, hastily – why halve it?

They, apologetically – sorry, they'd sent the wrong letter that time. Posts were so uncertain. Purely an official mistake, they meant double it. I could take 100lbs of luggage.

Myself, by telegram – what is the uniform?

They, at length, sent a fascinating picture of the uniform and an imperative telegram to depart at once. 'Should I ever be like that elegant young woman in the picture?' I wondered with a sigh as I packed my small belongings for the longed-for land of France. For once I felt almost as big a fool as all my friends believed me. Who but a fool gave up the comfort of a feather bed and a quiet home for all the dangers of France? But the neighbourhood believed me a heroine of the first water. Old ladies, with tears in their eyes, implored me not to be too rash in the firing line, and the Laird of the district sent his own motor car to convey me to the Station. So – not knowing in the least what I was going to do, where I was going, with only my telegram of summons, the uniform and a pink chiffon frock which, as a forlorn hope, I had packed at the last moment – I set forth.

Notes

1. 'The Army brother' was Christina's brother, David Barrogill Keith, known in the family as Barr. Two years younger than she was, he served with the Scottish Rifles during the war and was awarded the Military Cross.
2. Scapa Flow, just north of Christina's Thurso home, was the UK's chief naval base during the First World War.

2

Delays at Headquarters

First stop London, that was clear enough. The Department airily explained they had only meant 'come to *London* at once'. I could not possibly get to France for another four weeks yet.

Myself – aghast – where could I stay?

They – vaguely – oh! That hadn't occurred to them, but if I made a point of it, there was a hostel down Islington way. I could try there. But first of all – this with great firmness – I must be photographed. Tottenham Court Road – top floor – Jew – at once.

As I laboured up endless flights of dark and dirty stairs, I still found one subject for thankfulness. What a mercy the folk at home couldn't see me now! At the top I was taken charge of by a metallic looking woman. 'Passport,' she snapped. '3/6d. – Hat off, full face, keep still,' – all at once like a machine gun. I had never been so photographed before. No brush! No comb! No mirror! A blinding flash, then her voice again. 'Ready in three hours. Goodbye.' I reflected it was just as well I had been accepted for France before people saw my photograph!

Islington I had never visited, but in the daylight it was not so hard to find. Yes, I could be taken in on Saturday for a fortnight. That was the men's section next door – they had all sorts, from a Catholic bishop down to a chimney sweep, all together. The women were nearly as mixed. I loved the brown walls, the quaint cretonne curtains, and the cups and saucers – orange-and-black patterned on a background of cream. The windows looked out on to a quiet old market square. Islington must have been delicious when it was a village.

Had I been inoculated? Vaccinated? No – then both at once. Mayfair was the best place. So away I trudged. The Mayfair waiting room reminded me of Maple's showroom, and the doctor, I decided, must be treated with remoteness and severity. He looked as if he might wish to flirt.

At length – weary and rather cross – I betook myself to a friendly boarding house in Willesden Green. France seemed years away and I thought it strange of the Department to send me to live in a slum and to be inoculated in Mayfair. But I did not know Departments yet – it was my first day in London.

3

London before embarkation

How hard it is to leave London when one has been there even for only four weeks! I love it, I love it, I love it, from the people in the buses to the waitresses in the tearooms. Talk about the Navy being mystified about why I was going to France! Why, everyone here looks on me as perfectly wonderful because I happen to be going at all. Even in the dull old boarding house — how did I ever think it dull? What interesting people there were! A newspaper woman who wants me to write on 'Thrilling Days in France', a diminutive medical student who tells me how best to nurse my arm when the inoculation begins to throb, a self-denying barrister – quite good looking – who stays nearly three hours late from the Admiralty in the mornings just to comfort me on these same occasions, another woman who actually told me that all the men think I'll be a great success in France (they haven't seen me in my uniform yet) and last but not least a grim old Scotsman who gave me a packet of lozenges when he heard me cough. 'Leave me your address,' said he, 'and I'll send ye a tin of oatcakes when ye get oot bye. It'll mind ye o' Scotland.' And Plum-Leaf Villa, said the landlady herself, would always have a room for me, when I was passing through on leave. Not bad for four days in a totally unknown boarding house!

The next event was the Islington Hostel. After much labour in the total darkness I reached it and found I had staggered up with my bag to the men's section.

'First to the right,' came a cultured Oxford voice in greeting, 'and I will take your bag.' At any rate I had not struck the chimney sweep, I reflected, and wondered if it was the Bishop. But, Bishop or chimney sweep, I guilelessly confided my bag. To my surprise a very substantial dinner – when dinners were hard to get – awaited me in the women's section, and sent the women flying up in my estimation. After long and painful experience of College life, I had ceased to expect from any purely female establishment a decent dinner.

After dinner, however, came a heart-to-heart talk. I suppose it had to be. I discovered that nobody but myself in the company was going out for Educational work. We included a serious and spectacled young person who'd done Rescue Work for nine years and looked it (I'd rather be on the streets than be rescued by her!), an ex-Music Hall star who'd been out with a Lena Ashwell party and had the widest vocabulary I have ever heard, a Canadian VAD [Voluntary Aid Detachment] – six months' service in Salonika and disillusioned about all mankind (capital 'M'), an Irish mother and daughter going to run girls' clubs in a Naval port (lucky Naval port!), one dear nurse invalided home from Mespot – best of the bunch she was – a Chaplain's wife carrying on for the Chaplain and taking no Bible lessons from anyone, thank you!, and a very pretty runaway from Cornwall dying to go to France.[1] She and the Chaplain's wife had cubicles next to mine, and the heart-to-heart talk found and left us, from diverse reasons, dumb. But after the first night we became great friends. It was all through my hot-water bottle which burst at midnight and in bed the very first night we were there. Shivering in my nightgown, I surveyed the damage. I had always been told it imperilled one's life to sleep in a damp bed, and mine was swimming. But don't you believe it ever again. Oh, the things I had to learn when I went to France! Squeeze the blankets, lie on the pillow and bury the sheets and you'll sleep better than you ever did before.

Well, in this zoo for a fortnight on end we were lectured on things we ought to know in France. Not me, of course – nobody knew what I was going to do, so how could they tell me what I ought to know? Still, the others might have to do pretty nearly everything, it appeared. Stock and run a canteen, hold an impromptu religious service to suit any variety of denomination, umpire all games from football to billiards, work a cinema lantern, lecture on and settle all or any labour disputes. They learnt it all in a fortnight though you mightn't think it, and I with them.

The only part I remember was 'How to treat the Army' for that was where I began to take notice. 'Always back up the CO,' said the Sergeant, 'and never salute him. Whatever he says tell him it will be done. Don't bother so much about the Adjutant, he don't matter so much.' I saved that one up for the Army brother, an Adjutant himself.

'Always be neat and tidily dressed, no matter what you're doing.' I remembered this when I was called upon to sweep a chimney. 'The men have got to be neat and tidy and they'll think less of you if you're not. Never grouse. Do everything you're told.' It sounded like the Ten Commandments.

'And when the men grouse to you, don't let 'em run the War Office down. As long as you're in France; whatever you think, it's the best of all possible War Offices. And, drunk or sober,' the Sergeant finished his address, 'the men are top-hole men.'

At the time, the idea of any man being top-hole when drunk was new and alarming. But I've learnt better now. The Canadian VAD was sitting next to me. 'I like that – drunk,' she commented. 'A drunk Officer spoke to me the other day in Piccadilly. I spoke back to him and took him home. I'm going to have tea with him this afternoon if he turns up – I told him he'd have to be sober, though.' I gasped; speak to a man in the street! Only girls who were not nice did such a thing. She looked at me. 'You can take this from me. When a man speaks to you in the street, always answer back. If you don't, the other kind will.' Well, I hope I've learned that lesson too.

Then there were the study circles – quite a bit worse than the talks as nobody knew what to say, and so we gradually drifted on to social problems, where most of us had views. The Rescue Lady and the VAD were, of course, poles apart. For myself, the one time I spoke was when I suggested, as became me, that Education was the one remedy for the housing problem in the slums. It came like a thunderclap in the assembly and produced an amazed silence. Presently, however, the Irish naval lady gave out that it was the key to the situation, and thereafter the debate languished.

In the afternoons we went by bus or train to inspect canteens and camps. In the terrific scramble to get on buses, I remember with gratitude an ex-joiner of Herculean frame who always shot me aboard first of the throng in the midst of the astonished bus. And my arm being rather bad in those days, I remember too the busy waitresses who yet spared a minute to cut up my food, and the fellow travellers – particularly fat charwomen and rather grimy men – who took such scrupulous care not to jog my sling.

There were lighter moments of course, as when I had a heated skirmish with my tailor, who summoned two of his assistants to aid him, over the length of my uniform skirt. I won, and it remained one ninth of an inch shorter than regulation. Then there was the Department which suddenly discovered I was urgently asked for in France and that my French military permit was forthcoming in record time. Unfortunately, however, it had counted without the Voluntary Ladies' Department. Great war-workers these! Hours of eleven until twelve and two until four, Saturdays eleven until one. It was their duty to get our passports – gradually, of course. They had already taken three months considering the situation and were quite grieved that I wanted it now, or sooner, if possible. 'Ah, yes,' said the French Consul, as he added his visé, 'Zat is ze office where zey do nozzing right nevaire! Zeze ladies!' Being a woman myself I quite agreed with him that women never work as well as men. I've always known they were not half so pleasant to work for.

Still, the last day did come. My uniform was delivered, and with its tabs and cuffs and VAD cap it looked smart beyond words when I put it on. My fourteen photographs arrived to placate the French Government. I had been vaccinated and inoculated (twice). I was armed with the English passport and with the French military *permis rouge*. My ticket was in my hand and by the kindness of the Clerk at Waterloo Station to a somewhat lone, lorn female, with her heart in her mouth, I actually had a berth on the steamer for France.

We were a noisy crowd at the Station when the iron gates of the platform swung to between us and England. Americans with mountains of luggage, just like peacetime, were crossing to Paris. It was my first taste of Americans and I had yet to learn that it is their natural habit to shove and push. Some Scottish women next door were going to Servia, some English wives to Paris.[2] But in the long train I seemed to be the only British girl in uniform.

The crowds were worse at Southampton – much. We were penned into a little fold for four solid hours, while every document we possessed was examined by sleuth dogs. It was sheer luck I had my Food Card with me. I reflected I had not my Birth Certificate, if it occurred to them to ask for that. My luggage had long since been wrested from me. 'No return to the United Kingdom for four months,' snapped the very last official.

'A nice thing that,' I thought, 'to take away as a farewell when one goes to serve one's King and Country in France.' What price for education here.

To my surprise, they didn't search me. There was nothing else they missed. You couldn't have caught them out in any other detail, relevant or irrelevant, about me, from the shape of my nose down to my inmost motives for going to France. They had it all down in their books.

'Name and address of next of kin,' demanded the last official but one, 'in case the ship goes down.'

I gasped. Don't they just think of everything!

Southampton Water was blacker than the blackest of pitch when at last I was flung out on to the boat. At least, they said it was Southampton Water, though how anyone could tell beat me. My berth was the very lowest on the ship and she was the veteran boat of the line. The only ray of comfort was the news that a good dinner was then being served in the dining room. 'Now I'm in for it,' I reflected, after the cheering remarks of the Inquisitors. 'I'll have my dinner and be damned to them.'

When I came on deck again it was blacker than ever and we were off. An officer of the Silent Service, seeing me alone and I suppose looking frightened, came up. 'Put on your lifebelt and go and lie down. I'll come for you if we're torpedoed.'

So England said, 'Goodbye' nicely after all.

Notes

1. Christina's fellow residents at the hostel reflect some of the range of opportunities there were for women to be involved in war work. Actress and theatre producer Lena Ashwell organised small companies or 'parties' of singers and actors who went out to France to entertain the troops. The Canadian VAD, meanwhile, was part of a vast organisation of voluntary nursing assistants who served in military hospitals, often coming from upper- and middle-class backgrounds and with minimal training.

2. These women were probably going to Serbia with the Scottish Women's Hospitals, an organisation remembered for its outstanding work on the Balkan Front under the leadership of Dr Elsie Inglis.

4

France and her
welcome – Dieppe

It was a bright, crisp November morning and we were in port. Neck to neck with us lay one of His Majesty's own destroyers – grey and clean and bright. They said she had been with us all the time, but nobody could be sure of that. At any rate she was worth looking at until the French Authorities made up their minds whether they wanted us ashore or not. Apparently the Inquisition was massing again, ready to go one better than its brother in England. After all, in this time of war, how could it rely on its brother in England? How could it tell what we had been doing on the way across? We might have taken any amount of doubtful characters on board en route. So cross-examined again we were.

Set free at last, I discovered that all my French had deserted me. 'There's nobody here like me,' I said forlornly to a beautiful RTO [Railway Transport Officer] behind a red wicket window.

'Oh yes,' he replied briskly – taking me for a motor driver, 'there's one.'

A remarkably capable khaki damsel advanced upon me. 'Sorry I can't take you in my car,' she remarked. 'I'm full up. Where's your luggage?'

'In the boat,' I said hopefully.

'Pierre,' she called, and a fat blue-bloused person dived foremost into the hold. If they'd stowed my luggage as far down as they'd stowed me, he might be hours I felt. 'There's a tram here will take you to the station,' she went on, 'and you'll just catch the Paris express. Oh! That's right Pierre.' The tram lady grabbed me by the shoulder, my luggage landed after me with a resounding thump, and alone of the *Vera*'s passengers, I was off. So much for looking helpless and solitary.

'*J'ignore tout*,' I said in distress to the conductress – it was all the French I could muster.

'*Mais oui*,' came the sympathetic reply, '*C'est comme tous les anglais; c'est toujours comme ça.*'

['I don't know anything' ... 'Well, yes' ... 'Like all the English; it's always like that.']

It was well meant, of course, but not, I felt, complimentary to the country I was leaving. However, it made her all the more attentive to me. 'My three brothers I have lost,' her voice came placidly, 'My husband he fight. I work, you work – it is like that.' She seemed like the spirit of France as she stood there stoically tinkling her bell and carrying on and viewing with compassionate amusement such amateurs as me. I left her with a kind smile in her eyes, as an army of small boys surrounded me and my luggage at the station. Providentially I knew where I was going and they managed the rest. Except for proffering my bread card to the ticket collector, I made no more mistakes and found myself aboard the Paris express with orders to change at Rouen. It was like France to have the white lace still on the carriages and how comfortable and roomy the carriages were! No crowding and strap-hanging as we had in England! Normandy looked fair and peaceful – the farms well-tilled, the orchards rosy in the crisp, clear air.

All too soon we were at Rouen and in some trepidation, I descended.

My own countrymen, in masses, banked up the platform, and in smiling, welcoming masses too. I spoke to an air corporal near me. 'Your train will be that one over there, miss,' pointing to an engine steaming and puffing on one of the side lines outside the station. 'Better jump in before it comes to the platform.'

I stared at it aghast. A whole vista of railway lines lay between me and it. Trains were entering and leaving everywhere. 'But I can't cross these lines,' I stammered, thinking of our orthodox English Railways and their views on the matter.

'You'd better,' he returned inflexibly.

I had an inspiration. 'You come with me,' I suggested, though how that would make the proceeding safer, I did not reason out. It certainly took him by surprise, but in a moment he was down on the rails and I was with him. I thought of nothing but him as we crossed miles of rails. 'You get in here,' he commanded. It was impossibly high, but he was not to be baffled now. With one hand he opened the door and with the other he swung me up and in – head foremost – amidst a group of respectable English ladies en route for Dieppe. Collecting myself, I waved a farewell to him from the window, and turned to survey my companions. They had levelled a frozen stare at me of some moments' duration, but the stare, I found, was not caused by the manner of my entrance – which apparently was quite an ordinary one in France – but was due rather to my now dishevelled appearance. I was left to think mournfully of the Sergeant's parting advice always to appear neat and tidily dressed, as the train gradually approached Dieppe. I was very excited at the arrival. Beyond the stare, the English ladies had betrayed no sort of interest in me. Who would meet me? Nobody did, but the passport official took charge of me. He commandeered the English ladies to their surprise and told them where to set me down. The sea was breaking in clear, green waves – the clearest green you ever saw – as we drew up facing it, at the door of the Headquarters. I turned to look at it – the only thing I knew – before I went in to my work.

5

Life at a base – who wants to learn?

My first thought was – how pretty the Base is! – my second, how far away from the line, where I longed to be. Headquarters made me feel as if I had plunged into the ocean itself off the deep end, as the Army brother would say. A babel of tongues went on all around me – Australian loudest of all, and most of the speakers greeted one another by their Christian names – across the whole distance of the room. 'Nobody expected you by this train,' my guide said in a temporary lull. 'I don't know how you could have caught the connection at Rouen. Nobody has ever done it before.' They had not met my Corporal then, I reflected. 'You don't really belong here,' she confided again presently. 'This,' – with an air of dramatic importance – 'is the Headquarters for France. You go to the local Headquarters. Somebody will take you there directly after lunch.'

I felt remarkably cheered. College-bred as I was, I did not quite see how I could ever fit in with this menagerie. However, it's a habit one easily acquired in the Army.

'I'm going to Paris this afternoon,' said my other neighbour, helping himself loudly to coffee, 'looks like peace in the *Daily Mail*. I'm for Place de la Concorde on Peace night.'

'Take me! Me too!' came in chorus from all quarters of the room.

'I should love to go to Paris,' I said quickly.

My guide looked coldly at me. 'You can't get there without a special military permit — you can't get anywhere in fact.'

'How do you get, old boy?' queried one more quietly than the rest.

'White pass — on business,' came the curt reply, with a wink to help it out.

'He is one of the chiefs,' concluded my guide. 'His car can go anywhere.' I made a mental note that it was desirable to cultivate chiefs with white passes, if I wanted to see life. This one paid not the slightest attention to me — next-door neighbour and newcomer though I was — so I gave him up.

In a few minutes I was on my way along the sea front to the lesser glory of the local headquarters, my new home. In happier days an artist from Paris had built it for himself, with its wide windows looking far across the English Channel and its red roof snugly sheltered by warm wooden gables. He had left his tapestries and his old Norman china for us, plus the minimum of furniture and that of a highly artistic and rather uncomfortable kind.[1] We called it 'The School' out of compliment to the work we did in it and our motto was 'We live and learn.' Never was a truer device for the next — all too short — six months we had the luck to stay in it. What a merry life it was and what a gay one, and what strange wisdom we learned in the 'best school of all'.

The Chief, tall, dark with twinkling brown eyes, awaited me in his study.[2] 'So glad you have come,' he remarked to me over a litter of papers on his desk. 'You are the star turn allotted to this area. I understand you are capable of teaching up to the Greats standard in Oxford. I shall put it in Base Routine Orders straight away. English and French I suppose, up to any standard you like.'

By this time the 24-hours' journey, the cross-questionings and the lunch were beginning to take effect on me, and I wanted nothing but sleep, and up to now nobody had ever mentioned where I was going to do that. Perhaps it was like London, I reflected, and it hadn't occurred to anyone I would need to. Anyway, the recital of my qualifications now 'put the lid on!' I conjured up a vision of rows and rows of troops, all athirst for knowledge and finding out what a fraud I was. But the Chief was finishing. 'Miss Mordaunt will take you now to the Coq d'Or. I have engaged a room for you there.'

The Lady of the Lovely Hair — for so we always called her — was before me. Showers and showers of golden hair neatly tucked away, keen blue eyes, and capability in every inch of her figure, characterised Miss Mordaunt. Ability to get what she wanted under every possible circumstance, was one of her lesser charms. The landlady of the Coq d'Or was firm and uncompromising. '*Pas d'eau chaude. Que voulez-vous? C'est la guerre.*' ['There's no hot water. What do you want? There's a war on.']

I began to think we should be beaten. But not so Miss Mordaunt. 'Get into bed,' she said. 'I have a Tommy cooker and we'll get a hot-water bottle straight away.'[3] I needed no second bidding and, grimy, tired, travel worn, anything but a star turn, I fell sound asleep with Miss Mordaunt's hot-water bottle clasped in my arms. Time and again since then it has been her fate to find me 'down and out' as on that first day and to send me straight to bed. Across the world as she is today, I doubt it never can happen again.

And then work began in real earnest. At least, it would have, if within a week the Armistice had not stepped in. I knew it first by the *bonne* bursting into my bedroom with the shrill cry '1870 is avenged!' The tumult in the street outside was an echo of her words. A statue of France with a broken sword stood there down in the public square below me, in memory of 1870, and round it all day long surged cheering crowds.[4] The statue itself was smothered in flowers, November though it was. Only the figure of France could be seen standing breast high in a sea of roses. '*Les voilà, Mlle*,' went on Germaine. 'Even the English officers are dancing.' They were singing and marching too in serried rows down the Grande Rue.

We saw no *poilus* but French marines, with that odd red hackle in their caps, walked arm in arm with Belgian troops. From the pavement stolid groups of Chinese, cabbage in hand, surveyed them curiously. A dark French Senegalese soldier from the Military Hospital on the *Plage* jogged past a Portuguese – worst behaved of all the Allies and sent here to be shipped home as soon as ever occasion afforded.[5]

'Aux armes, citoyens,' they played over and over again and I had hardly got over the marvel of the 'Marseillaise' being played for 'peace' when, faint and halting at first, but more confidently as it went on, the strains of 'Tipperary' rose to my ears. They had not played it much since 1914, but it was the first thing they thought of today. 'It's a long way to Tipperary, it's a long way to go.' The Band went on – a French band – playing 'Tipperary'. But it was useless. If the 'Marseillaise' failed to suggest peace, 'Tipperary' called up only 1914 – the August days of it. All day long the surging crowds cheered round the statue. 1870 was avenged.

At the School alone, there was quietness. The roll call of the classes fell away by one half on Armistice night and hardly ever afterwards recovered. Late in the afternoon I went into the huts to see the men and how they took it. The Base Commandant had sent round word to close the canteens if we wished, as the men might be drunk. But we did not wish. On that night of all nights every man, drunk or sober, was to find a welcome there.

When I went in, they were still sober and the hut was packed to the door. Most of them were singing and some few laughing and talking. Would you like to know what they sang? No 'Rule Britannia' or 'God Save The King' – English soldiers rarely sing either unless they are bidden. No – it was a chorus we were to hear every day for the next six months, with varying emphasis – 'When do we go home?', each word punctuated by thumps of mugs on tables, and the last word raised the roof.

At night they were many of them drunk, and the sober ones, with thoughts of the punctilious WAACs [Women's Army Auxiliary Corps] with whom they were dancing, were for turning the drunks out.[6] 'No, no,' said the Hut leader firmly, 'let the drunks dance by themselves in this corner.' So, sometimes three together, sometimes the orthodox two, sometimes one, the drunks danced merrily in their corner; whenever one, well meaning but nothing more, lurched out to grab a WAAC, he was hastily but tenderly shepherded back by a stronger comrade.

Outside bells blared; flags flew; bands played; at every window in the Grande Rue faces looked out, laughing, crying. In the distance the 'Marseillaise' came rolling down and its echo 'It's – a – long – way – to – go.'

I stole into the Cathedral. Over the altar hung our flags, quiet and still. There was no need to wave them now. Utter quietness here and one spot of light only. In the chapel at my side lay the empty tomb and the marble watchers beside it. The figure of the risen Christ was outlined and ringed with light. Never have I seen so many candles ablaze together. Beneath Him in the darkness knelt clusters of black-robed women. Peace had come.

Down by the shore the water was quiet. If only there had been a destroyer on that clear green sea, I could have believed that peace had come. But having lived for four years beside the Grand Fleet, I found it hard to believe that anything great could happen and the Navy not be there. It was *Hamlet* without the Prince.

Still, here we were at Peace, and the Army had to be taught until it went home. More than ever now as its proper work was done. But the Army wanted home straight away and sooner if possible. We held a council of war. At present we had only Base Troops and when Demobilisation came, these would soon have their hands full. Also, their heads were none of the best, at any time, or they would not have been at the Base. So our thoughts flew ahead. Would we get our chance with the fighting troops in the Forward Armies? They were the goal of all our hopes – night after night I went to bed and dreamt I had really met them. Well, meet them I did eventually – but not to teach. To flirt with, yes, for whirlwind weekends, and nobody in the world ever flirted quite so well as they did, and then, standing on the pier with unresponsive France in the background, I waved them off to Blighty. *Sic transit Gloria Mundi.*

In the meantime, whom could we teach? No one was forced to come to us except from a few camps in the area, where the Commanding Officers, possessed by a zeal for education, thought it desirable to send their men down in lorries to classes as a parade. From reasons hardly the same as those of their Commanders, the men too thought this a capital plan! First of all it exempted them – which was in itself a benefit – from a severe Physical Exercise Parade; secondly it gave them an enjoyable motor excursion from the desolation of the mud-flat that was their camp to the bliss of a real live Base; and thirdly it gave them a whole hour at their own sweet wills in that Base. It was true that for one hour, too, they had to sit on benches before an Instructor at 'School' and profess a desire to be taught something, but even that was not without its entertaining moments.

Well do I remember being sent to find out what one set wanted to learn. 'I wants to write a letter, Miss,' began Private Nobbs, a middle-aged man of disapproving aspect.

'But surely you can do that already?' I returned in surprise.

'No, Miss – that 'ere little writin' I means – same as likes of you puts and 'ard to read like – not them big letters same as mine.'

This somewhat daunted me, it being the only compliment my handwriting has ever extracted, but outwardly I preserved a business-like calm. 'Writing class,' I jotted down. 'Report to the Chief at the end of the hour.' Alas for my compliment! At the end of the hour Private Nobbs, seeing the Chief's handwriting – even more illegible than my own – decided he would prefer to model himself on that. I tremble to think what stage of development his calligraphy may now have reached, for he went for the writing lessons as, had he only been younger, he would have gone for the Boche.

Private Wooley, his neighbour, was a very superior person. 'I wants English literature,' he said haughtily.

I took a deep breath. 'Yes?' I said enquiringly, balancing my pencil in my fingers.

'For to be a reporter-like to them newspapers,' he went on.

I thought of Lord Northcliffe and waited expectantly.[7]

'I wants to write police reports – can make a good bit o' money that way.' *News of the World* – I made a note. I had no experience of writing police reports myself – it not being included by the University of Edinburgh in their curriculum of English literature – but I knew the kind of thing this man wanted.

'Write an account of a drowning accident for me,' I said promptly and passed on to the next.

He was an old soldier – served his time in the regular Army long years before the War and was really too old to have been sent even to a Base. Still he was there. He began the conversation. 'You be the fourth young lady we've 'ad, Miss,' he said encouragingly, 'and all of 'em larning their job.' This was somewhat dismaying, but I reflected that all troops learned French as a matter of course and that was probably how he had had four of us.

'And which of them do you like best?' I questioned, ignoring the second half of his remark.

But he was not to be caught. Quick as a shot came the answer, 'We allus likes the last 'un best, Miss,' which, I think, under the circumstances, could not have been bettered.

'And what do you want to learn?' I pursued.

'Not partickler, Miss,' he replied amiably, 'anythink you likes.' Being of the old Army he, like his superiors, did not hold with Education, but it gave him an hour at the Base, so he came.

A bespectacled youth, converted by the war, wanted to learn the Greek Testament although he could not even ask for it grammatically; a good many wanted shorthand – one man quite genuinely asked for sewing – but the general demand was for anything that would pay after the war. As we styled it in our official communications, the demand was 'vocational'.

One night the corporal in charge of one of these lorries came to me in great distress. I gathered that he had arrived duly at 'School' at the appointed hour; it was a dark night and he was sitting beside the driver. When he got out to disembark his men, not one of them was there. 'Started with me, Miss, they did, all of 'em. An' to go a-wastin' of your time like this,' – he was speechless with indignation – 'an' givin' me the slip too,' he added sorrowfully. 'I'll dish 'em – I will, when I gets 'em back.'

The Chief was never surprised at anything. 'Go and round them up through the town, Corporal,' he said, 'and fetch them here for their lesson – they will have it right away and no town leave.' I confess my sympathies were all with the truants who had noiselessly escaped from the lorry and the vigilance of the Corporal just as they entered the town.

Apart from these parades, however, which were productive of very little good, as the men's hearts were rarely in their work – apart from these, we had the voluntary classes both at 'School' and in the camps themselves. To every camp round about – and there were many – we sent out instructors. Once a week as a rule they came in to 'School' to report. Camp life was delightful and everybody loved it. Being considered a star turn, however, I was held to be too important to be wasted on an outlying camp, and except for flying visits to each and all of them, I was retained at the Base.

The delightfulness of Camp Life – as any woman would understand – lay largely in the fact that you were the only woman there. You interviewed the General – if you were Miss Mordaunt – for a hut for your classes, and on the same condition, you got it. If you were a male instructor, you only reached the Brigade Major, who might possibly promise you a hut in the dim future. But, being Miss Mordaunt still, you got the Brigade Major to help you find the hut and Staff Captains galore to have it fitted up for you. But then few of us had, like Our Lady of the Lovely Hair, the privilege and pleasure of being six weeks in Camp with the Guards' Brigade, which in itself was an excellent training.

Then there was Circe, dark-haired, white-faced, fascinating. It was a very muddy camp that she was sent to – for even in mud there are degrees – and after a week she failed to report. But not so her Camp Commandant. 'The camp was knee-deep in mud,' he wrote, 'the lady had arrived, it appeared, in the daintiest of tan suede shoes, fresh from Bond Street. Consequently after one day, her feet had crocked. The Principal Medical Officer spent most of the morning bathing them, while the Commandant's entire Staff was occupied in amusing the lady for the rest of the day.' Plainly the CC [Camp Commandant] had not himself fallen a victim. And it was very like Circe to have the Principal MO [Medical Officer] in attendance as distinct from his subordinates.

The Chief was not amused. 'I will recall her at once,' he said, ordering the car, 'and shoes or no shoes, she shall come with me to the RE [Royal Engineers?] stores and be fitted with military boots – regulation pattern.' And, though you might not think it, that was not the last of the tan suede shoes. They provided her with riding lessons from a compassionate Major of the camp, who thought it would be so much better if she hadn't to walk at all, and they formed the subject of a severe order to all future ladies of England who might think of coming out to us – nothing but boots of the heaviest pattern would do.

For myself, I was sent up to a Remount Camp to find out if anything could be taught there.[8] It was a small camp and very outlying. Later, in a different guise, I was to revisit it. The men in civil life were mostly grooms. I went into the Hut to talk to them and they affably made room for me in a big circle round the fire. I tried to find out where they came from – chiefly the Midlands and the backwoods of Yorkshire. They politely asked if I minded them smoking – which I did not – and the remarks of the Yorkshireman were translated to me by his more civilised-speaking companions. But the visit, though pleasant, was non-productive. 'Fact is, Miss,' said the spokesman, in the tones of one arriving at a happy conclusion, 'we don't want to learn nothink here, we don't. Not but what we'd like to see you, Miss,' he gallantly hastened to add, 'every Saturday night, when the car comes.' But I reflected that a 'star turn' would hardly be allowed up every Saturday night for conversational purposes, and I knew that in any case, any power I had in that direction, would rapidly give out.

Rarely have I done anything so difficult as give a lightning sketch of English literature to men who have read nothing but sundry and rare passages of the Bible and the racing columns of the yellow press. Between their knowledge and mine a great gulf stretched. For them, it entirely passed their comprehension how anyone could be interested in a novel. Yet when, omitting all literary references, I told them the story of *Beowulf*, they asked for more. Alone of all the camps in the Area, this one unabashed for many months chose to remain in its blissful state of ignorance. Eventually, when even we were being demobilised, it suddenly professed a passion for arithmetic and actually did advance laboriously as far as vulgar fractions. The decision to learn, we found, was the thought of one bright spirit who hoped they might thus be able to circumvent the War Office in its nefarious designs – which of course were unquestioned – of docking arrears of pay when they were being demobbed. Spurred on by this hope, the whole camp devoted itself with acclamation to its arithmetic.

Circe had been replaced in her camp by a solemn young man who, as might have been expected, made no progress whatever. On the contrary, in addition to the rapidly dwindling list of would-be learners he forwarded to us every Saturday, he went near to losing the Hut itself. An overflowing canteen demanded it and the CC granted their request, and after an interval, provided for us a damp tent insecurely anchored in a sea of mud. After that, with what we considered astounding suddenness, under the circumstances, the attendance went galloping up.

'Better go and see what's happening there,' said the Chief to me one day with a puzzled frown. 'How a soaking tent that is half afloat can round up crowds like that, I can't understand.'

It was indeed half afloat, I realised, as I waded knee-deep through the mud, only hoping that the wind would not blow me headlong into it the next minute. I arrived at the tent – the guttering oil lamps had gone out and by the light of a single candle, the solemn-faced young man was propounding theories of the most advanced Socialism, thinly veiled as Social Economics. He regarded my arrival as inopportune. To do the men justice, they were just as ready to ridicule his points as to praise. They knew it was a forbidden subject, so human nature being what it is, they flocked to hear. To tell the truth, they never liked men instructors at any rate, and ours were never plums.

The solemn young man was hastily withdrawn and the Camp Commandant, being now very prickly – and righteously so – the Chief decided to send him Miss Mordaunt. It was a masterstroke and we had no more trouble there. When next I visited that camp, I crossed to the tent by a neat path of duckboard: there were chairs and a stove in the tent and oil lamps burning brightly – another tent next door served as lecture room, and both tents would have been huts, had not Miss Mordaunt intimated to the Camp Commandant that as long as the men were in tents, she preferred to be too.

Besides sending Instructors to the camps, we advertised ourselves and our classes at the School. Base Routine Orders were all very well, but they were the official organ and we were not at all likely to get eager students through them. So we made out bills – red and blue and green bills, with pictures, most enticingly got up. No such thing as English literature figured on those. I had learnt something from Private Nobbs. 'Come and Learn how to Write a Story,' and under that head I read or told how the few best stories in English had been written. 'French' did not need to be camouflaged as everybody – even the WAACs – wanted to learn it. But equally everybody thought a senseless language like that should be mastered in at most a fortnight. It was a clean waste of time to spend longer than that on it. 'German' at this stage nobody wanted to learn, though, when the occupation began, we had floods of applicants for even a week's course. The Irish Guards indeed, sent up unpremeditatedly to Cologne, wrote eagerly back to Miss Mordaunt for German grammars, so anxious were they to learn. Bookkeeping and shorthand drew well – a very practical and prosaic audience this. Nothing exciting was ever known to happen there, except once when a Pitman shorthand class was provided temporarily with a Gregg shorthand teacher and the resultant tangle had to be unravelled by main force by the wrathful and returning Pitmanite. Then there was the singing class. No shyness to come forward here. The Base Commandant led the way and the entire Base seemed ready to follow him. It is not often you get the chance of yelling louder than your Commander and not being punished for it. So the choir grew and multiplied with a will, both as regards numbers and lung power, until in the end we had to borrow a hall for it, as no single room in School – to our relief – would hold the singers. 'History' did not figure on any of the Bills under any disguise as nobody at the Base would ever consent to learn that. You see history consisted mostly of war and of that, past, present or future, they never wanted to hear again. The only exception was a small squat man, who came one late afternoon and asked for a lecture on Frederick the Great, to be delivered at once. That stumped us all. Eventually the Chief took it on as he had, in the remote past, done History at Oxford. He said that the man listened stolid and unmoved during the whole hour's discourse, and at the end, equally stolidly, picked up his cap and departed. We never fathomed why he had asked for it.

One item on the bills was 'Commercial Geography' and though the lecturer for it was one of the best and a distinguished member of a Home University Staff, it failed to draw. After some thought we changed its title to 'Mining Areas in the North of England', and the roll call leapt up. 'Applied Art' despite its dull title, was a great success – partly because of its first-rate teacher, in peacetime design artist to the best jewellers' firms in London, Paris and New York – and partly because in it the men were taught to make something and anything they did with their hands was popular. Where they failed, of course, was in intellectual flexibility but that was only to be expected. Just as 'Applied Art' drew crowds, so did 'Motoring'. The War Office handed us over an old car and every morning from 8 to 10, relays of soldiers and WAACs – all hoping to earn their living by their new knowledge in the peace world – were instructed in the mechanics of Motoring.

Whenever a subject grew unpopular, we camouflaged its title. 'How to Write Letters' and 'How to Make a Language' introduced the study of grammar. But you can't do much with Latin or Greek – they refuse to be disguised. Still, I had pupils for both, all the time I was there – few certainly, but very earnest. They would trudge on the wettest of wet nights for nearly two miles for a lesson on a Latin declension; they were all married men with families, printers, gardeners and the like, and they never missed a lesson all the time I was there. I think they wanted to learn because it was such a relief to get into a beautiful house, quite away from the Army atmosphere – we were not official – and to hear nothing but English around them. They also liked having Englishwomen to talk to and they had more chance of that at the School than at the crowded canteen. Finally I do think they liked Latin – at any rate they liked its logic and they loved the beauty of the Greek script. One of them used to make me the most exquisite Greek exercises, simply by copying out sentences he hardly understood.

There were a few freak turns too. There was the gentleman who came to learn the violin every afternoon and squeaked unbearably in the process above our heads, and the smart young motor-despatch rider – South-American born – who wanted to keep up his Spanish. He was a problem. Our Spanish master had left and nobody then on the Staff knew any Spanish. The Chief hated to say, 'No' and the boy was waiting. Such a nice-looking, pleasant-mannered boy! It was a shame to turn him away. I explained things to the Chief and he assented. So, with the boy's consent, I, not knowing the language myself, took on the Spanish.

Latin and French and likewise Italian were part of my 'star turn', so it did not take much ingenuity to learn a little more Spanish than he did. He could pronounce the thing and I knew the grammar and we got on famously. Latterly we used to read *The Scarlet Pimpernel* in Spanish together. It was the only book we could get, and he got it by scouring the whole countryside in his off hours on his motorcycle. Then there was the Australian doctor who wanted to learn Italian, as she was going to spend her leave in Italy, and who informed me with disgust on her return that she wanted no more lessons. Italy was a third-rate country and the Bay of Naples wasn't in the same street as Sidney Harbour. And there was the natty WAAC Commandant – also Girton trained – who came to read Italian, and the EFC [Emergency Fleet Corporation?] Captain who had been a year in Italy and whose Italian was better than mine.

But our prize lecturer was the philosopher who came out prepared to instruct the troops in the Psychology of Dreams. No one at all responded to his invitation on the bills, so we rushed him out to the canteens, on the well-known principle that if the mountains won't go to Mahomet, Mahomet must go to the mountain. Of him more anon.

Talking of canteens, every cinema at every canteen filmed our bills night after night, and that, we thought, was the very last thing in the Art of Advertisement.

Two other things there were, which made an invariable appeal to all ranks and conditions of the Army – they were Shakespeare and the Old Testament. I have had the most enthusiastic letters from quite unexpected units about *Macbeth*, as if Shakespeare had done them a personal favour in writing the play. It was never possible to obtain any Shakespeare books from the canteen libraries – so great was the run on him – and we were never able to supply sufficient copies from our own store to satisfy the camps around.

The case with the Old Testament was different. I had few books and the men had none. Yet for any study of English we must read something good. No English prose writer – though we had the choicest passages culled for us by Dr Hadow in the one book at my disposal – would hold the men for more than a moment. They were all voted slow and some dead slow. At last in despair I hit on some of the Old Testament short stories. The result was a *succès fou*. It did not come from familiarity, for until I told them, few had any idea what book I was reading. Even then, when I explained that it was the best prose in the world – irrespective of its religious merits – they were rather pleased with themselves for having liked it. So we abandoned with one accord the eloquence of Coleridge, of De Quincy, even of Charles Lamb – whom they plainly thought a fool as well as a madman – in favour of the real stuff purveyed to us by the adventures of Joshua and the like.

Notes

1. In the late nineteenth and early twentieth centuries, Dieppe attracted many artists. The house which Christina calls the School was known as 'Blanche'. It belonged to Parisian artist Jacques-Émile Blanche (1861–1942), and was nestled beneath the cliffs on what is now Rue Alexandre Dumas, overlooking that clear green sea. Blanche invited many models and artists to his home, including Renoir, and he photographed Degas here. The house no longer exists, having been badly damaged during the Second World War, but there is a photograph of it among the YMCA Archives. Male members of staff lived in the School, while Christina and the other women were billeted elsewhere to preserve respectability.
2. The Chief was the Sub-Director for the Dieppe area, Henry Brooke.
3. 'Tommy cooker' – a small portable stove used by soldiers in the trenches.
4. The statue in memory of 1870 by sculptor Eugène-Paul Bénet is in the Place des Martyrs in Dieppe.
5. '*Poilus*' were the French infantrymen. Although she writes with her customary sense of superiority to all other races, Christina's description does emphasise the international nature of the Allied presence in France.
6. The Women's Auxiliary Army Corps was a voluntary service established in January 1917 to free men up from non-combat roles such as cooks, telephonists and clerks.
7. Lord Northcliffe was the leading newspaper magnate of his day. As the owner of *The Times* and the *Daily Mail*, he had huge political and popular influence.
8. Remount Camp – the Army Remount Service was responsible for supplying horses throughout the army. This particular camp was at Luneray, about 11 miles south-west of Dieppe.

6

Work and play

There is a wise old nursery rhyme which says, 'All work and no play makes Jack a dull boy.' Possibly the Authorities thought of that when they devised our life. At any rate they made our work as diverse as they could. As I sat one morning poring over the Chief's mess accounts, I thought to myself that I still could not answer the query of the SNO at home – 'Whatever are they sending you to France for?' The school was empty, for it was after 10 and the men were away at their military duties. I was now billeted in a French family, and only the men Instructors, as well as the Chief, lived at the School.

It was thought a bright idea by the Chief that I should run the Mess and look after the French servants. Considering I had spent all my life being looked after in Universities, it struck me as rather funny. But I tackled it gaily. The Chief little knew that he was confiding his welfare to a Bluestocking who had never cooked a dinner in her life, and whose knowledge of how porridge should be made depended on what she remembered from the choruses of Aristophanes. But, being Scotch, she did know how it ought to look. 'Our porridge is like soup,' complained the Chief bitterly. 'Marie Henriette might as well serve it up with the dinner.' But Marie Henriette knew the technique and I the results desired, and after we had experimented one morning with a will, I decided the last way would do. The following morning, pan in hand, she met me at the School door. The pan was empty and she waved it like a flag. 'The *Messieurs* have eaten all.' So that was that.

Our rations arrived in an old Ford car driven by Uncle Joe, a misogynist, who would never see me but who consented, under protest, to communicate with Marie Henriette when necessity arose. Usually he arrived at break of day, rattled up the *chaussée* to the old back door, dumped down the rations outside and speeded away. It required the utmost vigilance on the part of Marie Henriette to collar him at all – yet collared he must be when he forgot such things as our jam or our bully beef.

When, after a sleepy breakfast in bed – my Madame preferred it thus – I strolled down to School about 11 a.m., I descended to the kitchen regions and surveyed the rations. At first Marie Henriette, bag in hand beside me, explained volubly how far they would go and how she had been compelled to supplement them. 'Monsieur A has desired this,' she declared, 'And Monsieur B – he so love that.'

I cut her short and let it be known with rapidity and precision that her one care in life was to be Monsieur Le Directeur. '*Pour ces autres*,' I went on, '*ce qu'ils veulent, ça ne fait rien.*' ['As for the others,' ... 'what they want does not matter.'] I waved my hands airily and thought of *ces messieurs'* faces had they heard me. But the morning I came upon Monsieur B, with his head bent over a dictionary remarkably close to Marie Henriette's, must have been a red-letter day for them both. She was very handsome and he was irreproachable, our dream philosopher, Lecturer on Psychology and all the rest of it. Furthermore, they were both of them married and old enough to know better. But, as far as that went, I was a don myself and for the time being, mistress of the house too. So I faced him. Summoning up my courage – Marie Henriette having discreetly wilted away – I told him flatly that I would not have him flirting with the servants. He returned with some heat that he had not been flirting and then I suggested sweetly that in that case he should continue his French lessons with the ladies on the *Plage*. He was beaten and he knew it. Only once again did I catch him out and that was the night he was leaving us. When coming to say, 'Goodbye' I found him in the dark kissing Marie Henriette by the kitchen door. And so French had I then become that I thought it all in order and turned the other way.

But if the kitchen was out of bounds to British troops, it was by no means out of bounds to those of Britain's ally. Marie Henriette was understood to have a husband somewhere. 'Marry perdoo,' quoted the Corporal tersely who gave me her particulars when I engaged her. Marie Henriette herself, more warily, only spoke of him as '*disparu*', though she styled herself quite complacently '*veuve*'.

But what she lost in a husband, she made up in brothers. Of her and none other might the song have been written 'An' if ye lose yer mother sure it's hard to git another – but it's easy for to git another man, Mary Ann.' All ranks and conditions of the French Army would congregate in the School kitchen. Latterly I would not have turned a hair had I met le Maréchal Foch himself between the Maconochie and the bully beef on our kitchen table.[1] And Marie Henriette had one order for them all, as I came down the stairs. '*Debout,*' she would call in a stentorian voice, and a flashing row of be-medalled and be-ribboned *poilus* – and sometimes officers – confronted me. Marie Henriette led me down the row as the inspecting general. 'Michel, *mon frère*' was from Verdun, three times wounded, Croix-de-Guerre – incidentally he had today brought us the butter from Marie Henriette's country home. 'Auguste' was older – he wore the *fourragère* and was himself commanded to explain to an ignorant person like myself what that stood for. Fine-looking, handsome fellows they all were and not one of them failed to salute me when we met afterwards in road or street. Indeed – through Marie Henriette – I said, '*Bonjour,*' as regularly to French troops as I said, 'Good morning,' to our own.[2]

I can still hear the little refrain the Staff hummed a propos of that, about me at the School – the days it had had a good dinner! '*Très chic et magnifique, et toujours très jolie*, the soldiers cry as she goes by "*Bonjour* Marie".' For the sake of English morals, I had better explain that my name neither is nor was Marie, but the words were taken from a song then very popular in the canteens.

If my views of the French Army were coloured by Marie Henriette, hers of England, I discovered, were a startling reproduction of the Base. It was a country where, wherever you went, there were all husbands and no wives – endless Messieurs in becoming uniforms who spent most of the day in making love to you – their money was unlimited and they spent it without a thought and a grateful country provided them gratis with their food. '*Ah, Mlle – que je voudrais bien aller en Angleterre,*' ['How I would love to go to England']– and she said it as if it were heaven. No doubt far and wide in France today, the impression is the same. Well, she is in England now, but her luck has held. She is keeping house for a bachelor in Piccadilly – so probably she is still quite unaware that there are '*mesdames*' in England.

It was drawing near the end of November and the Chief felt a 'star turn' should not be kept doing accounts – however precisely she totted them up – nor yet hunting up a laundry which professed to restore one's own *linge* [linen] instead of conducting its affairs on the diverting but precarious Bran-Pie system. 'Take a dip, take a dip in the old Bran Pie, you may get a … you may …

or even a Commission in the Coldstream Guards.' On Monday mornings Monsieur B, our philosopher – the beloved of Marie Henriette – talked with affectionate regret even of English laundries by comparison and a propos of this, he one day asked me if I would have a prescription made up at a French chemist's. His own French, he went on to explain – no doubt owing to some failure of my efforts, I inferred – had not progressed far enough for this. Such of his shirts, he assured us, as had come back from the wash, had been sent back in a tub. He was delicate and did not wish to catch pneumonia. Indeed, it was because he had been unable to stand the English Winter that he had thought of coming to France. 'This is a far, far better thing I do,' murmured the OC Stores [Officer Commanding Stores] – a friend of mine who was lunching with us – 'than I have ever done. I go to a far, far better rest than I have ever known.'

So I spent that afternoon trudging from chemist to chemist. Apparently the prescription contained a drug unknown to France. But I would not go back without it. 'Put in something else,' I said to the last chemist wearily, 'it's only for a cold,' and a mythical cold at that, I said to myself.

Nothing loth, he obeyed. French chemists are not like English ones. 'If the monsieur drink much of this,' he said placidly, corking the bottle, 'he grow ver' seek.'

'Not poison?' I said in alarm.

'But, on the contrary, *Mlle*,' he waved his hands, ''e grow well, but 'e grow seeck.'

'Excellent,' I said briefly, 'it is what is to be desired.' It was after this that the Chief sent me up to the Camp where they 'didn't want to learn nothink', to take over the canteen for a few days. I heard on my return that nothing but the best cognac – and lots of it – had been able to restore Monsieur B, who firmly believed I meant to poison him.

The stores and I went up to Luneray camp together – I sitting beside the chauffeur, the nephew of a bishop in England. This was exciting because, as he explained to me on the way up asking for my sympathy, there was a regular old standby lecture on 'Some Bright Spots in England' delivered by an earnest padre at every camp within hail. A few of the Bright Spots, such as Wakefield and London and Sodor and Man had added luminaries in the way of Bishops, and when they had, the orthodox son of the church did not hide them under a bushel. To give the desirable homely touch indeed, he always pointed out, as one particular Bishop was shot across the screen, 'that a nephew of his lordship drove the Stores car that they knew so well.' This was the men's Bright Spot and made the rafters ring.

'If he weren't such a darned ass in any case,' said my chauffeur bitterly. 'I'd — '

'You mean the padre of course?' I enquired innocently. He turned and looked down at me speechlessly. 'Don't do that,' I said hastily, 'or we'll go into the poplar trees straight away. They think of everything in France you know. I've no doubt Napoleon even thought of you and me when he planted those fringing the road.' I hope the Bishop, his nephew and I don't ever meet together in England. I should instantly think of the Bright Spots and then I shouldn't behave as the Bishop would like.

It was five o'clock when, with many a gasp and heave, the Ford at length pulled up at Luneray. It was on the heights – remote from any village or hamlet. It commanded the English Channel and had William the Conqueror's Forest behind it. They said that while the Conqueror was riding through the forest one day, the thought came to him that he might occupy England. And so he did it. As simple as that. Anyhow the Forest was worthy of the thought.

On the crest of everything stood our canteen. The men's huts were dotted all around. I hastily donned an overall and got behind the counter – for the first time in my life. Pouring out mugs of tea was not so bad, nor yet giving the change therefore out of five franc notes (it being payday at the Camp), thanks to the French Government's admirable system of decimal counting. But the canteen's ration of tobacco had arrived with the Stores and the queues stretched right to the door. The orders came something like this: 'Two teas, Miss, and two packets o' biscuits – sweet ones if you've got 'em – three and two packets o' Twist, six packets o' Woodbines and a tin o' Soldier's Friend.'

'Only one stick of Twist,' I said gently, 'and two packets of Woodbines – we're rationed you know.'

'Very good, miss,' he said obediently. 'Tea and Twist and as much chocolate as you can give me and a tin o' Soldier's Friend.'

'Of what?' I said mechanically counting out the chocolate.

'For cleaning buttons, Miss – on the second shelf on your right,' prompted the next man in the queue.

'No, Miss, you ain't got none of it. Ain't been none of it for the last three weeks, there ain't,' said another finally, with keener eyes than mine for what was on the shelves. 'Tea and Twist and 'arf a dozen candles, Miss.'

I looked up in surprise. 'It's only two I've been told to give,' I hesitated.

'That's right, Miss,' came the steady answer, 'but I comes from Sainte Valerie, bit o' ten mile off. We gets six all right, Miss, as we ain't got no canteen there.'

Never once have I known a soldier take advantage of a greenhorn behind the counter. The Prince of Darkness is a gentleman but, although the Saints might tempt you to believe it, he is not the only one. The British Army – other ranks – are there every time.

This was a Remount Camp on pay night. In the hut the men were packed like sardines in a tin, behind the counter there was no one but myself and I was hardly the experienced elderly person that was *de règle* for this canteen. But there wasn't a man I didn't talk to, as well as serve, from 5 to 9 that night, and some few, remembering my last visit, had a special welcome for me. 'Come to stay, Miss, 'ave yer this time – come for keeps?' I shook my head sadly. After all, an elderly lady is hardly very exciting if you want to sing, 'If you were the only girl in the world' as they were doing then.

At last it was closing hour and they melted away and I turned exhausted from the counter. The Quartermaster was beside me. 'You'll come and 'ave a bit o' supper now, Miss.' In the little room behind, 'tea and something with it' was laid out for me.

By ten o'clock I was very sleepy and in my head was still doing sums. *Tea, Twist, three boxes of matches, two packets of Woodbines* ... 'Where am I going to sleep?' I enquired lazily.

The Hut Leader was clearing up. 'Oh, didn't they tell you?' He turned round. 'There's a hoose in yon wood aboot ten minutes' walk from here. I'll tak' you roond whenever I've finished this.'

'They won't all be in bed will they?' I faltered, wishing I was there. 'I hope it's not too late for them.'

'Them, them,' he repeated in surprise, 'Lassie, there'll be naebody there but you.'

I jumped. 'Alone in a house in the wood?'

'Ye'll be a'richt,' he went on, putting away the last dish. 'Ye're no feared, are ye?'

'No,' I said boldly. It wasn't done to be 'feared' in France. I sat in silence.

'If ye have a hot-water bottle by ye,' he went on, 'I'll fill it from the boiler and ye'd better tak some caunles. There's nae licht in the hoose.'

Nothing worse could happen now. I opened my suitcase and gave him the bottle. 'There's a wee jug owre there,' he said, pointing to the top of the boiler. 'If ye like to tak some hot water wi' ye. There's nae fire in the hoose.'

I hadn't been with the Army for nothing – I obeyed. 'There *is* a bed in the house?' I said anxiously, as he opened the door.

'An a fine yin that,' he returned with great heartiness. Outside it was pitch darkness – worse than Southampton pier. He went first, with the can of hot water and my suitcase. I followed, with a lighted candle and my rubber bottle. We hoped the candle might burn, sheltered by his back, as he was not very sure of the way. It did not. Except for the wind, there wasn't a *human* sound anywhere. Who would have thought there were thousands of men in huts quite close? By the time I had bumped into the second tree, I began to think less of William the Conqueror and his forest.

My guide turned aside. 'This isna the right way,' he said cautiously. 'I'll haud by the left till we get to the path.'

'Here we are,' he announced cheerfully in a minute, as I went over the knee in mud and spilt most of the hot water in the process. 'There's a gey lot o' mud here,' he said, sensing the catastrophe. Fortunately it was not all quite so deep, but as long as you were in the midst of mud, it appeared that you were on the right way. At length there seemed to be fewer bumps and I felt, rather than saw, a house loom up. It was quite a considerable house – a 'shatoo' in fact, as the troops called it, by daylight. 'There's an orderly sleeps in yon stable,' my guide pointed out. 'Ye'll no be feared if ye hear steps like, about five in the morning.' Dumping down the can, he produced a key and unlocked the door. 'Ye'll be a'richt now,' he sighed, when all my belongings were inside. 'Guid night then.'

'No, no,' I cried in alarm. It was pitch dark inside too and I could not find the matches. 'You come and see that it's all right,' I pleaded, 'Look in the wardrobes, and … and … behind the doors and under the beds.'

He seemed surprised, but did as he was bid. It was very daintily furnished, but I was in no mood to appreciate it then. We creaked upstairs together. My bed was, as he had said, fine, and the bedroom was beautiful. Off the dressing room was a wide balcony, simply made for people climbing up but I could do nothing about that.

'Ye're no really feared,' my guide said at the door with the candle, now lit. He said it as if it were incredible.

'Not really,' I said, 'but I can't come down again to lock the front door. You do that and take the key with you. And if I don't come down to the Hut by 9 tomorrow morning, you're to come and fetch me – promise you will.'

He was a complete stranger, a man that until 5 o'clock that night I had never seen before in my life, and here we were, standing together in a bedroom in a lonely house in a wood. He held a guttering candle – which was our only light – and wore a puzzled frown on his face, as he looked down on me. I still hugged a hot-water bottle with one arm, while the other I had laid on his coat sleeve to emphasise my requests. I have since thought we must have made a dramatic picture, had anyone looked in. The only moral thing about us was the fact that the door was open. In fact, all the doors were open – even the front one, wide. 'Guid night,' he called again, clanking cheerfully down the stairs.

As he turned the key in the lock below, I locked my door hard and then looked round my big room. One candle makes a very little light and a very big shadow. I could not very well undress in the bed, though I should have wished to. It seemed the safest place. But just as at Southampton, a happy thought came to cheer me. 'Well, if I'm killed, or – even frightened,' I said to myself, 'the man who does it will be lynched – torn limb from limb, in fact.' This was very comforting. 'The Remounts will see to that all right.' Then I saw the fun of the situation. Here was I, all alone in a lonely house, with not a creature near, and locked in too! Anything might happen – even anything nice! It was the comfiest bed I have ever slept in in all my life and I didn't even hear the orderly at 5 a.m.

Next morning my boots presented a difficulty – they were a rich khaki colour – mostly all over, though here and there, faint streaks of black – their intended colour – could be seen. However, they were the only ones I had, so I put them on. Being locked in, I had to get out by the window, and as I climbed up to the canteen, voices from all quarters – tops of trees, roofs of huts, insides of lorries, far down the horselines – greeted me with 'Good morning, Miss.' If it had been the Queen herself, they could not have given a heartier welcome.

The Hut Leader was just serving breakfast. 'A wis just comin' for ye,' he remarked. 'What's the matter wi' yer airm?'

'It went septic,' I explained. 'The vaccination, you know, and when the bandage came off, madame poured ointment on it – tons. But it's clean now. The English MO has bandaged it and he says it's doing beautifully – it's stiff today,' I added, 'because there were such a lot of mugs last night.'

He looked unconvinced. Hut ladies usually have stronger arms than that. I rather liked talking of my arm. He held the frying pan suspended, while he looked at me. 'D'ye mean to tell me ye've been vaccinated?'

'Of course,' I returned in surprise, 'we all had to be.'

His mouth set, 'A don't hold wi' vaccination myself – it's a perneeshus idea – in fack,' he went on slowly, in a burst of confidence, 'a went once in a deputation to the Pope to protest agin it.'

I gazed in wonder. What had the Pope to do with it anyway?

'But, if ye hev been vaccinated,' he said regretfully, 'ye'd better put this on it,' producing a small round box. 'A invented it masel. It's nine times stronger than iodine,' he finished impressively.

'Good Lord,' I cried in alarm, pushing away the box. 'I – I daren't take off the MO's bandages,' I went on, after a minute. 'He's trying something special with my arm, but thank you all the same.'

'A sell lots of them to the men,' he continued, 'they'll ask for't at the counter.' He was quite right – they did, often, but all the same, I did not put it on.

We ate our breakfast in silence – he being Scotch, was no talker and I was afraid to speak for once. At the end he rose. 'Can ye sweep a chimney?' he enquired slowly. I'm afraid I looked blank. Pursuant to the Sergeant's instructions, I had done up till then everything I had been told, but I didn't even know how to begin this. 'Weel, weel,' he said with a sigh, 'a doot a'll hae to do't masel, but ye'd better bake some shortbread for tea, a'm expectin' the Chief.'

My heart leapt. How nice to see the Chief again! *He* hadn't asked me to sweep chimneys. But my host was speaking. 'Ye'll mebbe no' ken how to make shortbread, like?' he enquired tactfully. I did not. In self-defence, most Oxford dons don't. 'Tak' off your boots and put on your overall an' a'll show ye.' We didn't make real shortbread, not having the ingredients, but a kind of Quaker Oats cake, crisp and sweet and brown – rather easier to make. At least that is the only way I can account for my being able to make them – after only spoiling two. Never have I passed a happier morning and when at 12 o'clock, I hurried to the counter to serve the first cup of tea, my cheeks were hot, my hands were floury and I expect, so was my hair. But the troops were not to be daunted. 'You looks like a little bit o' home, Miss,' one said in plain tones of admiration. 'Don't she just,' echoed the Quartermaster proudly from the depths of the orderly kitchen.

'Ye'll no' be forgettin',' said the Hut Leader to me at lunch, an hour later, 'that this is St Andrew's nicht. We'll ha'e a supper after nine o'clock in ma room.'

It was indeed 30 November – tho' I had forgotten it. This was, I suppose, why the chimney required to be swept. It was the quaintest St Andrew's night supper to which I have ever sat down. To begin with there was no whisky – not that I would have drunk any in any case – but it seems to go with St Andrew. The Hut Leader and I had the honour to represent Scotland – the Chief was English but well intentioned, and so was the Quartermaster.

We dined off chestnut soup – made from chestnut flour specially sent out from Gibson's, Princes Street, to the Hut Leader – then roasted chickens – the *pièce-de-résistance*, those, and produced from somewhere by the Quartermaster. 'However did you get them?' I said in admiration. We usually dined off bully beef or fish, when I could get it.

'Well, I points to what I wants, Miss, and then I say "*Vous blaguez, Madame*" when she sez the price and there it is.'

Dessert was my cakes and the canteen chocolate, and then in lemonade we drank 'Them That's Far Awa'.

After that the Hut Leader announced that the Camp Commandant had invited us both to lunch on the morrow – and what about my boots? The Orderly had expressed a desire to clean them. 'But,' I exclaimed in distress, 'even if he does, they'll be muddy again before I get to the Camp Commandant.'

The Quartermaster intervened. 'I'll find you a pair of gum boots and you'll put them on till you get to the CC's house. Then you can put on your own at the door.'

It is not the usual way of calling at home – to put on one's boots in the porch – but I did not want to disgrace the troops, and when I did get as far as the CC's dining room next day, he could have seen his face, had he chosen, reflected in the polish of my boots. It was a very stiff luncheon – all prunes and prisms – the CC treating me with withering politeness from behind the majesty of his eyeglass. Just once again I saw him, down at the Base, cantering a fiery charger through the crowded Grande Rue, and clearing it before him. It was on the tip of my tongue to shout out, 'Halt' and I knew the horse would have pulled up dead. But the consequences to me would have been – well – undesirable, though not unexpected.

As we walked back from luncheon, the Leader told me a padre would arrive to conduct the service in the Hut that night. Now padres – bar one – are the only 'duds' I ever struck in France. This one was harmless. I was conducted to a seat in the front row, beside the Hut Leader, and the men were told they might choose the hymns. They had come in, mud-soaked and fresh from the horses, and were sitting patiently but wearily round. It was perhaps natural, I reflected, that they should choose 'Days and Moments Quickly Flying' but I only really understood the reason when we came to the rousing chorus of another hymn 'And nightly pitch my moving tent – One day's march nearer Home.' I think the padre himself must have been surprised at the fervour of that last line. I endured the sermon with the thought of the next hymn. It came – one of the old Glory hymns – 'Wash me and I shall be Whiter than Snow' with the 'Wash me', as the Army would say, in triplicate, at the beginning. When I stole a look at the mud-stained, unkempt rows – it was not a 'parade' service – I could not keep the ghost of a smile from my lips, but I hope it was a kind ghost, for I loved the singers.

But the regulation lady was coming back, and in a few days I had to go. I have seldom been sorrier leaving anywhere in my life than leaving Luneray. After the first night in my house in the wood, I felt just like an Enchanted Princess with all my Knights round me. To the outside world they might be rough and horsy and stupid, but I knew they were gems – tophole, as the Sergeant had said

– every one. There they were, on treetop, hut roof, far down the lines, waving goodbye as the Chief and I sped away.

Down at the Base it was work again. A very important Visitor had arrived from England – to organise correspondence work with the Forward Armies. The Chief was closeted with him for hours and then they sent for me. 'I feel,' said the Chief, 'that this will really be worthy of your talents.' I never quite knew how to take statements like that, though I am sure there must be a right answer somewhere.

The Visitor looked at me through his glasses. 'I am very much astonished,' he said severely, 'that you are doing so little at the Bases. I have been over them all. And yet the newspapers at home show that the troops are simply craving for Education.'

'Not the Base troops,' I said gravely, thinking of the Sainte Valerie lorry and its missing load.

'That's what they all say,' he returned, nettled. 'Why shouldn't the Base troops want it?'

'Because they are mostly no good in the line, you know, or too old to go up, and they all have their work too. They haven't much time for education.'

'Come, come,' he said, 'all the young officers are University men – everybody knows that – and *The Times* says they read Plato in the trenches.'

I was politic. 'We haven't those here,' I said.

'I come from Cambridge and I know dozens of young officers,' he went on. 'Where are they?'

Well, I came from Oxford, but I wasn't going to tell him that. 'Mostly dead,' I answered. 'They've won the war you know.' He must himself have been indispensable – he was under age – for he turned to his files.

'I have here a scheme,' he said icily, 'for instructing by correspondence all Units not in touch with a Base.' My heart leapt – teaching the Forward Armies! That was business indeed! I was prepared to love our Visitor, in spite of his *Times*. 'The men will write to you and say what they want (a little envelope for that). You will have a list of all Tutors available in France, with their qualifications, and where the subject has no Tutor, you will write to me (big envelope for that). I have all the Universities in England behind me and most of the leading commercial men in London. If music is required, I have a Tutor in Trinity College, Dublin.' Ireland all over, I thought, to choose a subject like that. Music by correspondence would hardly appeal, even to the Forward Armies. 'And you yourself,' he concluded, 'will undertake the classics, I believe.' I bent my head. 'It's a first-rate scheme,' he went on, 'and I think you hardly realise out here how interested people at home are in this demand for Education. Here I have overworked business men giving up their spare hours to this correspondence work, that the men may get the best of everything.'

'And so the men should,' I put in quickly, 'but you know, those you want to get at have no spare hours at all.'

'I fear you lack my enthusiasm,' he countered.

'No,' I said sadly, 'only your optimism, but I will do my best.'

'I have to go home myself,' he went on regretfully, 'as I cannot be spared from my present work – so I shall have to leave it to you.'

'Shall we get the bills and – er – envelopes and prospectuses printed then?' I suggested, hoping to change the subject.

'No,' he said curtly. 'I shall have those done in London. It will be quicker. We work day-and-night shifts there, you know. And I'll send them out by a friend of mine, who is just going back.' Probably one of the dozens of young officers, I reflected. It was. And he dumped them at Boulogne whence, because of the severity of the weather and the bulkiness of the packages, I could get no car to retrieve them for weeks and weeks.

When the Visitor had departed, we breathed again. Oh! I had one parting shot at him. 'I could give you final instructions,' he said to me, 'about the manner I wish this done, if you come round to the General Headquarters tonight after dinner, about 9 o'clock, say.'

'I am sorry,' I said quietly, 'but I teach from now on till 9,' – it was very nearly teatime then – 'and I have to have my dinner after that.' What the troops would have said – or done – to him, if they'd heard him suggest I should walk along the *Plage* by myself unescorted to see him, at 9 p.m. I did not say. He might be spared that, I felt, seeing he knew so little already.[3]

At tea, the Staff waxed very merry over my new job. Any of the local officers – and all visiting officers – were welcome to drop in to tea, and most of them did. The Chief, his secretary and I, the Philosopher and the OC Stores, were the only permanent members in for tea. Between them, they devised a new title for me – 'OC Odd Subjects, Lonely Soldiers' Department, Care of British Army.' 'Care of British Army, anyhow,' said the Philosopher bitterly.

'You will have to give up housekeeping now,' said the Chief, I trusted with regret, 'when you go to General Headquarters. I have always hoped you would get something good like that.'

'But I needn't give up my classes, need I?' I enquired, in alarm. 'I don't want to be writing letters all the day. I'd much rather talk to the men.'

'You will have a secretary,' said the Chief quietly, 'but you needn't give up your classes. I will keep you for those.'

'What about our Christmas dinner?' said the OC Stores, suddenly. He had not spoken till then.

'I would love to do that,' I put in meekly. 'Couldn't I just do the Christmas dinner?'

'There are no turkeys in the Area,' said the Philosopher. 'All bought up by the Camps long ago – none in the market either, or likely to be.'

This was alarming. 'What about plum puddings?' I said to the OC Stores. 'Can you do them?'

He shook his head. 'I might do you about four,' he said, 'but each is only for one person. I need all the rest for the men.'

It appeared the Chief wanted to ask at least sixteen people, so four small plum puddings would be worse than useless. Suddenly I thought of the Quartermaster at Luneray with his '*Vous blaguez, Madame*' – he would wangle the turkeys for me, I knew he would. 'I'll do the Christmas dinner,' I said, 'and "twill be the nicest you ever ate.'

All the same, for the next three weeks, I was none so sure of that. But everyone played up. Marie Henriette took the most enormous interest in it. Her menu would have satisfied the Savoy, but we cut it down. She shook her head over the turkeys. '*Pas de dindes,*' she said, '*Messieurs les officiers anglais les out toutes, mais des oies, de belles oies.*' ['There are no turkeys,' … 'the English officers have them all, but there are geese, lovely geese.']

'*Non,*' I returned calmly, '*des dindes, deux,*' – for I had written to my friend. Sure enough a scrawl came down, 'Turkeys have been secured as requested, same to be delivered without fail on 23 December. P.S. Do not tip the bearer.' Indeed, we were the only mess at the Base that had turkey for its Christmas dinner. The plum puddings were beyond hope, but Marie Henriette declared she could make a chocolate cream that would make us think of heaven. Only, it required a dozen eggs. 'Impossible,' I said. 'We cannot afford that, even if we could get them.'

'*Mais non, Mlle,*' said Marie Henriette agitatedly. '*Il y a un de mes frères …*' [one of my brothers …] The French Army, it appeared, in the person of Marie Henriette's 'brothers' was willing to contribute the eggs. They were unobtainable in town. 'Also, *Mlle,*' went on Marie Henriette, warming to her task, 'there is *le gui* [mistletoe]. *Messieurs les officiers anglais,* how they love that!' She turned up her eyes. Marie Henriette had been cook to an officers' mess before she came to us, and she did not let us forget it.

'Yes?' I said doubtfully. It was well not to encourage her on some points.

'Michel, *mon frère,* he bring a cart load of it and *messieurs les officiers* help *Mlle* to pin it up' – planning it all out.

'What about holly?' I enquired, but she had never heard of it. *Messieurs les officiers* had no use for holly.

In the end there was a reunion in the kitchen; all the family came up from the country with the Christmas provisions. There was golden butter – precious as gold – with a cow carved on it, eggs galore in basins and a perfect forest of mistletoe, with Michel's laughing face peeping out amidst it. In the corner, were the turkeys 'as per order'. Upstairs a cataract of coloured paper and lanterns and flags had arrived – the gift of the OC Stores. It being an Allied undertaking, I handed over a Union Jack and a couple of Irish harps on a bright green ground to Marie Henriette for the kitchen. The two last, being those of an unknown Ally, proved a mighty distraction for the French Army. Upstairs I set the Philosopher to hang up the lanterns and the paper and the flags – not trusting him with the mistletoe.

'Can you get any wine?' said the Chief to me anxiously. 'The shops have none.' I knew that, but on Armistice Day, in my billet, Monsieur had produced champagne – which I had tasted for the first time in my life – and we often had cider. I still remembered Monsieur's toast – '*À tous ceux que nous aimons and à tous ceux qui nous aiment*' ['To all those we love, and to all those who love us']. I always think of it when I see champagne. Perhaps we would get some wine from him.

'I can get it *Mlle*,' he said politely, 'but it will be *prix de fantaisie*.'

'*Ça ne fait rien*,' I said gaily, '*c'est Noel, Monsieur, et la paix*.' ['It doesn't matter … It's Christmas, *Monsieur*, and Peace.'] After all, *vin rouge* and cider at five francs a bottle for the one and 50 centimes for the other would not ruin us, and the Chief had said I could pay what I liked for them – he would give it.

On Christmas Eve, we had a surprise. Uncle Joe wheeled up to the back door with 47 plum puddings instead of the four we'd been promised. England, alas! is always better than her word. I was helping the Philosopher to decorate and the '*officiers anglais*' (a gay party) were aiding the secretary to hang up the mistletoe when the Education Officer arrived with a large box. 'Going on leave tonight,' he said cheerily, 'but I've brought you a Christmas present – crackers – you never thought of them.'

'Oh yes, I had,' I answered, from the top of a ladder, 'but they don't run to them in France and it takes months to get them from home.' I fixed the last lantern and jumped down. 'You're a perfect dear, give our best love to England.' The crackers would be a lovely spot of colour at everyone's plate tomorrow, I thought. But I thought too late. Next morning, bouquets of red carnations arrived for each of us, from the officers of the Base. It was clear that the English officers appreciated us. I never see red carnations now without thinking of Christmas at the Base.

Just before we went in to dinner, Marie Henriette and I went round the table. There was mistletoe on the oranges and trails of mistletoe in straight lines on the table – trust France for straight lines. At each plate was a cracker and at each woman's place, a bouquet of red carnations. The *vin rouge* was there and the cider – its delicious yellow. Marie Henriette and her two French assistants were to serve the dinner, and as it was to be an Allied function and we had no orderlies, I decided the Philosopher must wait. He made a born butler and perhaps enjoyed it all the more as it necessitated visits to the kitchen. The OC Stores – as fitted by his office – took on the job of Footman. 'You'd better hand round the forty-seven plum puddings,' I suggested, 'and prevail on the guests to eat them – otherwise we'll have them every day for a month.'

So ended my housekeeping labours – with a blaze of glory on Christmas Day. In the evening we went to the Huts to help the men have an English Christmas. The Hut to which I went was a few miles out, at Rouxmesnil, and it was larger than most and possessed a cinema. For the first hour or so, we were fully occupied in serving out the tea and buns and extra fruit provided by the Hut Ladies, and then came the games. An eager throng surrounded me, pleading that I would come and watch a boxing match which was to be fought at one end of the Hut. Feeling it might be the least of many evils, I went down. A chair had been set for me, on which it was proposed that I should stand, at the inner edge of the ring. I got up on it. The preliminary skirmishes of the combat began. I had never seen a boxing match before, but they were not to know that. It is an exciting event, as I realised by the surging crowd pressing up behind me. I began to feel rather lonely on my perch. When the champions really did box and the crowd forgot all about me, what price my chair? A soldier with a garland of mistletoe in his cap stood beside me. I placed my hand on his shoulder strap and did the same to my neighbour on the other side. The hero of the mistletoe was immensely flattered. He stood like a rock. So did my other rather squatter pillar. The fight began. After the first five seconds I shut my eyes tight. The noise reminded me of a Rugger match in Oxford and I wondered if this would last as long. At any rate, I must stick to my post. Presently, at the sound of applause, I cautiously opened my eyes. The champions had finished one bout and were resting. I addressed what I hoped was an intelligent remark to my friend of the mistletoe. So intent was the ring, it had not remarked my eyes were shut. Three and yet four bouts succeeded and still the mistletoe man and I were there. But alas! for my hopes! In the fifth bout, the champions reeled up, interlocked, so close to my chair, that they cleared the entire audience around me. In an instant I had leapt from my chair, and was back amongst them, leaving the mistletoe man aghast by the post of honour. The attention of the audience was diverted at once. I was encouraged from all sides to return. The unfortunate champions were reproached. Feeling rather hot, I went back. But now the audience had two things to think of – which of the champions was going to win and when I was going to spring from my chair. The mistletoe man rallied me nobly. 'Don't you worry nothink, Miss, I'll stand by ye.' The champions, feeling they must recapture attention, in this laudable aim approached as near the chair as they dared. It was a new game, and even I was enjoying it.

At length a fresh thought struck the troops. How nice it would be to dance! Now dancing in the Huts, during the War, was strictly forbidden. They knew it. But the War was over – a month ago – and it was Christmas night. Still there was another barrier. A Hut Lady ranks as an officer and so is forbidden to walk or to dance with a private soldier. They knew this too. But it was Christmas night and the war was over. A third objection – had they known it – was that, personally, I had forgotten how to dance. But the eager throng now surging round my chair was in no mood to be refused. The Hut Ladies had already reminded them that dancing was impossible – I was not a Hut Lady – would I not dance? I was still standing on my chair and hundreds of hands were lifted pleadingly to me. Would I not come? Please, please do come. Never surely was the proudest ball-room belle in England so humbly begged for a dance. I thought of all those who had swept past me in balls in England. Would that they could see me now! Then I gave one hand to the mistletoe man – as he was still beside me – and jumped from my chair. I was ready to dance.

The piano was ringing out 'When Irish Eyes are Smiling' to the measure of an intoxicating waltz. But the pianist was hastily ordered to stop. The audience of the ring had no intention of watching the mistletoe man and me treading a measure from which they were excluded. They clamoured for the Lancers, as, in that, I realised, they would all actually dance with me. It was not that they thought anything of me in particular, but they had not been allowed to dance with an Englishwoman in France for more than four years – and in that state of mind any Englishwoman is a goddess. I am quite certain that each one of them imagined me to be somebody different, whom he knew at home. We began. Now I am small, and they were all rather large. Furthermore, the Lancers as the British Army – Other Ranks – dance it, is a highly rollicking affair. In this famous first set, I was the only woman on the floor and we soon were the only set. The Hut, as I have said, was large, but it was nothing for my partners, as we set to corners, to fling me the whole length of it. I trembled at the thought of Grand Chain. The mistletoe man was the strongest there. He was also, it appeared, the least expert dancer. 'Yer dunno 'ow ter dance,' he was told wrathfully more than once as we collided with the next couple.

'I darnces it as they does in London,' he retorted. 'I dunno 'ow they darnces it 'ere. It's all right, Miss,' he explained amiably to me. 'I knows the London way and they does the others.' The London way turned out to be all push and go, and I gave up all hope of trying to restrain him. I was thankful when, at the end, I could slip behind the counter and recover my breath. We had made wild dashes into all corners of the room, we had rushed up, whirled down, spun round, leapt up – but at least we had not fallen.

I began to pour out mugs of tea, thankful for the respite. To my surprise, a small crowd was gathering round my late partner. Some time after – when the Hut Ladies were now dancing and the floor was full again – he came up to me. 'Sorry I knocked yer about, Miss,' he said. ''Opes I didn't 'urt yer. Them other chaps sez as 'ow I was rough with yer.'

'Not a bit of it,' I consoled him. 'I think we took up a little bit too much room, but that was all.' I hope it was as a result of the dance that I was invited up to Rouxmesnil to teach French two nights a week after this and to go up each time in the Hut Ladies' car.

But now I had to move down to General Headquarters for France. I was installed in a beautiful big room on the first floor, directly opposite the Education Chief himself.[4] My room possessed two windows facing the sea and a large stove, which was carefully lit for me every morning. This, in the days of fuel shortage, was in itself a tremendous benefit. In the Local Headquarters, so minute had been our share of fuel of any kind that we sat about in greatcoats, except when the men had classes and we burnt our ration. Latterly, I got some wood through the Quartermaster, but it refused to burn in our stove. Many a time the Philosopher's cry rang through the house, 'Marie Henriette, *le poêle allé premener,*' which was discovered to mean 'the fire was out'.

Not only now, though, had I a fire to myself – I had also a telephone and many empty cigar boxes of the Visitor's. The room, naturally was of his choosing. I should not have had such an important one myself. His name, too, in black letters on white, flourished on the door though he had only occupied the place for a couple of days. My first care was to obliterate the name – no easy task. 'How did he get it on?' I enquired of Buttons, who answered my ring.

''E put it on 'isself, Miss.'

'Oh did he! Well, push some brown paper over it and write my name on that!'

The telephone at first was a great joy – it was English and in direct communication with HQL of C [Headquarters Lines of Communication]. I began to think of the interesting people I could ring up in my spare moments. Alas! That seemed to be the job of the other end. No sooner had I got well down to a letter than the telephone bell would ring, and Buttons' voice from below, 'Captain Brown on the telephone. Shall I put him through, Miss?' Captain Brown was our Liaison Officer at HQL of C – we were not Army proper – only attached to it, and he was the method of attachment. He was a young man who took his duties most seriously. I never saw him smile. He occasionally whizzed in to see me, rattled out his business, obligingly listened to my – I am sure – inadequate replies, and whirled out again. The one definite impression I could gather from him was that he preferred me to the Visitor, and perhaps that I was not such a fool as I looked. He voiced it better than that, of course, but that was what he meant.[5]

Next door to my room (GHQ had been, in peace time, a first-class hotel) was a magnificent bathroom complete with bath, into which about midday real hot water would flow. It was the first real bath I had seen since I came to France and I determined to take advantage of it. 'Buttons,' I said firmly, 'I am going to have a bath. If Captain Brown rings up say that I will see him in half an hour.'

Buttons was quite unperturbed. 'Very good, Miss. There is an extension in the bathroom Miss. Would you like me to put you through there? The Chief often speaks to Captain Brown from his bath.'

No doubt he did. But I wasn't going to. I should laugh in the middle of the conversation I was sure, at the thought of the immaculate Captain Brown at the other end and how shocked he would be if he could see me now. Up till then our interviews had been of the most proper, and I decided that for him, anyway, I should wear the white flower of a blameless life.

My secretary, too, was another joy at first. She was a remarkably pretty young woman who arrived with pencil and notebook at 9 a.m. prompt and seated herself opposite me with a vista of empty cigar boxes between us. After the first day, I put up a barrage of flowers which was not quite so depressing. At any rate, it did not suggest 'the morning after the night before'. But the pretty young woman could not spell – not a little bit – not for little nuts. It would never do for the Education letters to go to the Detached Units – from Brigadiers downwards – with phonetic spelling. Why, they might even want to copy it, as Private Nobbs had wanted to copy my writing. I saw the organiser.

'What a pretty girl you've given me as a secretary,' I remarked with truth. 'It's an awful pity to waste her on me. She's having such a dull time, poor dear. Look here, can't you shove her on to one of the men – they'd love her – and give me a plain one, the plainest you've got.'

He looked doubtful. 'The Visitor chose her,' he said. I gasped. So the Visitor was human after all. 'She *is* pretty,' the organiser went on, after a minute, musingly.

'Pretty,' I echoed. 'She's the prettiest girl in GHQ. What about the Chief with the white pass – the one that goes to Paris – he'd like her.'

'That's an idea,' said the organiser briskly. 'So he would. Well, I'll see about it. I'll send you in Miss Randel – she's plain enough to be a good foil.' I was left wondering which of us had won. At any rate Miss Randel could spell and worked like an automatic machine – we got on swimmingly all the rest of the time.

The work was really interesting. I had files from every one of the Forward Armies with demands for every kind of subject. The man who wanted to learn watchmaking by post was the greatest optimist – I had to break it to him gently that we could not teach that. The musical gentleman in Dublin wrote to me frequently and at great length to explain that organ theory is best taught by post and could I not find him pupils. But we were not allowed to suggest to the troops and none of them thought of organ theory for themselves. At times we really did begin to tap the University class of officer, but as soon as I got the Tutor fixed up, the officer was demobilised. I would receive a polite letter of thanks from Birmingham or from Birkenhead. The letters from the 'Other Ranks' were much more friendly in tone. They nearly always sent me their 'kindest regards' and on occasion their love and almost invariably began 'My Dear'. They were not even daunted at my sternly official replies 'Dear Sir' and 'Yours faithfully'. The next letter, on the contrary, would be even warmer and they always thanked me for my trouble.

When a letter came from Cologne asking for advanced mathematics by correspondence, I made a guess at why we were so popular. I happened to know that instruction in this particular subject could be had at Cologne from the Army itself – but this, as my correspondent explained, was just what he did not want. 'We have enough of the Army – we want something unofficial. You know more and you will help us more.' That was the gist of many of my letters. They were right about the quality of the instruction available. The names on my list of Tutors – at our Bases, and if necessary, in England – were amongst the most distinguished that England could produce. Never again, I suppose, will there be such a many-sided array of experts at the disposal of the troops. It is only right that I, who had dossiers of the qualifications of each of them, as no other had, should make this fact known. And the troops got all their instruction gratis. This too, they one and all appreciated. Many a time they said and wrote to me, 'We'll never get the like of this again, for nothing.' And they never will. A guinea an hour is what they would have had to pay in England.

But now that the Army of Occupation was more or less settling down, we were told that the Army there would teach itself – we were to restrict ourselves to the Army in France. Many a regretful note I had to send and receive from the Army of Occupation. And the Army in France was being demobilised – and quickly too. Our work was petering out. Only the local work with the Base Troops was really important now – as they would be the longest in France. We were a Demobilisation Port, and troops en route for England usually remained only three days – of that more again.

One fine morning, however, my old Chief sent round for me. 'I have some work for you,' he said, 'if you can take it on. Do you know who have arrived?' I shook my head. 'The Glasgow Highlanders,' he told me, 'at Arques-la-Chapelle, six kilos from here. They've marched all the way from Mons and will be here for a month. Their Instructor has gone sick and they've sent Transport down for another this morning. Will you go?' Would I go! There was a twinkle in the Chief's eye as he spoke. 'I daren't send them an English Instructor, you know,' he went on, 'Circe wanted to go.' She would, I reflected – new troops. 'But I said they'd like you best. Run away, the car's waiting.'

I needed no second bidding. In the hall I met the Philosopher. 'Where are you going to now?' he enquired. 'You've just come.'

'So have the Scotch troops,' I told him breathlessly. 'From Mons. And they've asked for Education before they've taken off their boots. Scotland for ever!' and I dashed off, leaving him perhaps a bit amazed. But once in the car, I began to reflect. I did not even know what instruction they had asked for. And if there was a whole battalion of them – in the open air! I had never taught Scotch troops before. All I knew was they would be different from English.

At length the car pulled up at the Camp and I went down the duckboard path. Short, squat figures in kilts looked at me cautiously as I passed, but no one said, 'Good morning.' English troops would have. At length I met the Adjutant, calm and cool. He produced some books – a very difficult and rather stodgy English grammar and a French conversation book. The men were in there – did I think I could keep order? They had never been taught by a woman before. Would I like him to be present – like a policeman, I said to myself. 'Oh no, thank you,' I laughed, 'I'm Scotch myself – I think I can keep order,' and I went in.

The men were sitting pretty well all over the Hut – many of them had replicas of the dull grammar, but most had illustrated papers, which they were hoping to read. At my entrance, the Sergeant called them to attention, numbered them off smartly, and presented two Companies for my instruction. He departed – I bade the men sit down, which they did in stiff rows. They stared at me in amused curiosity and their reluctant fingers played with their grammars. 'Come and sit nearer,' I invited. 'I can't see you over there. No – round this way' – as a man sat bolt in front of me. 'Now put away your grammars. We are not going to have any books today. Anybody here from Glasgow?' Three or four sat up. 'Well, I've sailed down the Broomielaw myself. But I don't come from Glasgow. Anybody from further North?' There were a few from Argyllshire, but most were from Lanark or Dumbarton. 'Oh!' I cried, 'I'm more Scotch than any of you. I come from north of Inverness.'

The whole class sat up. 'Ye're no Scotch, you?' one jolly-faced boy enquired incredulously. 'Ye dinna say't!'

'There's nane but English here,' came a miserable voice from the back row.

'Well, I'm not English anyway,' I answered cheerily, 'any more than you.'

'Ye dinna speak Scotch,' said a canny voice that had not spoken before.

'That's because I've been with English troops,' I lied bravely. Then I told them my name – it is an old and well-known one from Bannockburn downwards.

'Were ye at a Scotch University?' plied my last critic.

'I was,' I rejoined, 'at the best one.' They laughed. I had got them at last. 'Now,' I said, 'we're going to make a language – what kind of word do we need first?'

'Names o' things,' suggested one.

'Not a bit of it,' I replied, 'that wouldn't be much good for a grown-up person. That's for a child.' Volleys of answers came from all directions. Now it was awake, it was the cleverest troop class I had ever had. When it came to French in the next hour, I could hold them quite easily, textbooks and all. But with a new class – for the first hour – I never attempt to use books. We must get to know each other first.

Notes

1. Bully beef (corned beef) and Maconochie (a thin stew of turnips and carrots) were tinned staples of First World War trench food.
2. While the Croix de Guerre was a personal military award for bravery, the Fourragère was a braided cord decoration which was awarded to a regiment which had particularly distinguished itself.
3. Who was 'The Visitor'? As so often, Christina disguises identities – but she clearly thought very little of this man. There is a family story that Churchill visited and listened to one of her lectures, but she makes no reference to this in the narrative, and although it's tempting to think that the Visitor could

have been Churchill — particularly when she later refers to the cigar cases he left behind! — the details don't really fit. Albert Braddock, sub-director of Education based at Abbeville, referred to a Mr Fox who was involved in the correspondence scheme, so this may be Christina's Visitor, but we cannot be sure. His identity remains a mystery, just as she intended.

4. General Headquarters was in the Hotel des Étrangers, and the Education Chief was Sir Graham Balfour.

5. Christina's irritation with the telephone would continue throughout her life, and she had it removed from her home in Thurso when she lived there in her latter years.

7

Officers and men

When I first met officers at the Base, I was greatly surprised that I did not fall in love with them. I had been quite prepared to do so. It seemed only reasonable that I should. But I did not. They were so unlike what I expected them to be – old and prosaic and often distinctly ordinary.

The oldest and fiercest was a colonel who had been a naval officer, and, too old for that, he had been given a train-ferry job soon after the War began. His table was next to mine at the Coq d'Or, and the first time that he spoke to me, he told me in withering tones that he thoroughly disapproved of Education and of Classics in particular. He had learned the latter at Eton and, though he had been round the world in all sorts of guises, he had never found Classics the slightest particle of use. But behind his gruff manner he had the Navy's warm heart. Noticing my cough, he insisted on my trying a remedy of his own, and one night when I was hesitating at the door because the Church was crowded, he marched in with me to his own special seat.

The second disappointment was the Chaplain – a pukka padre too – who motored in from Tanks, shook hands with me with his gloves on, and then proceeded to cross-question me about my religion. He all but asked if I were saved and hoped patronisingly that I would enjoy my time in France, as if he were making a present of it to me!

'Why didn't you tell him,' said the Chief to me later, 'that you were really a Mahometan? He seemed to expect that sort of thing out here.'

And then there was the officer who invariably rode up to School though his office was only five minutes away. He rode badly, clanked up the steps in spurs, presented us with his photograph in riding kit and asked that it be hung up – prominently. He came so often and stayed so long, when I first went out, that I could not help getting to know him well. It appeared that he had a car, as well as the horse, and also a white pass, or its equivalent. Metaphorically I sat up. He could take me to Paris then! It appeared that he was quite willing. He was going for a weekend, anyhow, on duty. I rapidly counted out how long it would take for a letter to reach my sister in Paris to tell her I was coming. We were not allowed to use the French post, and the English mail was slower. Overjoyed at this sudden turn of events, I was prepared to look with kindness on the officer.¹

A day or so later I met Circe and told her I was going to Paris. 'With Captain S?' she enquired, without surprise.

'Yes,' I said. 'Isn't it fun? He's got a white pass and I shall see my sister.'

She looked at me. 'Nobody will believe that, you know. If you go with Captain S, you'll have to come back with a wedding ring.'

I stared at her aghast and then I felt myself grow red. 'But he's married,' I stammered, 'I know he is.'

'They all are,' she rejoined acidly.

I said no more, but next time I saw Captain S I took occasion to tell him quietly that I was not now going to Paris. 'Aren't you?' he said lightly. 'Well I'm not going either, as it happened.'

I soon received shocks enough to become disillusioned entirely about our officers. I ceased to take any further interest in them till Christmas, and agreed with Miss Mordaunt that Base officers by and large were 'like nothing on earth'. She, of course, judged them from the superior heights of the Guards' Brigade.

But, after Christmas, I revised my judgement – even of Captain S. It was bitterly cold and we had no fire at the School – hardly a blink of oil, even, for when the men came. I had to go along to Captain S's office one dark, wintry night. His office was at the top of several flights of stairs and I arrived wet, weary and cold. 'Oh, you've got a fire,' I said, as I stumbled in.

'Come along in and get warm.' He poked the fire – a real open English fire. He was Army, I remembered – not like us – and could indent for coal. 'You're wearing shoes,' he went on, 'and they're wet through.'

'We can't get them mended now by the Army,' I explained, 'and the French have only brown paper.'

'Well, I can get them mended anyhow,' he returned. 'I'll send an orderly round for yours tonight and have them done for you.'

'But it's only the RE people who can get them done,' I stammered stupidly.

'That's all right,' he said briefly. My shoes had many adventures. He gave them to an RE officer who gave them to his corporal with instructions to be 'done'. The RE officer was demobbed, Captain S went on leave and it was late in March before I saw my shoes again. But he meant well.

That night he trudged back through the sleet to School with me. 'There's something I want to show you,' he said abruptly, as we neared the door. In the midst of the storm he flashed an electric torch on the photograph of quite an ordinary woman and child. But he looked at them with veneration. 'My wife and little girl,' he explained. So I revised my judgement of Captain S. It was none so common to find an officer talking of his wife.

After Christmas the type of officer changed. Battalions began to be drafted down to our Area preparatory to demobilisation. A large demobilisation camp, capable of holding about 3,000 troops, was established close to our Base. All sorts and conditions of officers – from the Guards downwards – began to come to the School. They were all gay and carefree, some of them 'fey' as the Scotch have it. Their one object in life seemed to be to flirt with us. At first I was shocked – profoundly. In a crowded College life, one has hardly time to flirt, and I had never seen the fun of it any more than I had of dancing. So I sat in a corner and watched the Chief's secretary – who did it beautifully. But there were only two of us at School and they could not all talk to her.[2]

One, madder than most – merry blue eyes and daredevil manner – began to devote himself to me. He was so gay and I so grave that nobody believed we should hold together for more than half an hour. I would see nothing in him and he would soon be bored stiff with me. Well, we were neither of us bored, and with him I made the acquaintance of the cosiest little restaurants in the Base for tête-à-tête dinners. Sipping cider – I would drink nothing else – we talked of the good days that had come, with no thought of the past and none at all of the future. Sing 'A Little Cosy Corner and an Armchair for Two' and you'll bring it all back again.[3] Instead of heavy tramps through mud to soaking camps, I walked along the seafront with the Sainte Valerie lights playing on the green waters, and picnicked on omelettes and coffee at wayside cottages. There were joyrides too, when I was tucked up in a rug, with a hot brick at my feet and we went spinning along. After three weeks, he had taught me pretty nearly everything. Every prejudice I had started out with had been broken down. He set out to teach me to flirt as, in his opinion, what with

Colleges and all that, I must have had the devil of a time. I am generally fairly quick at learning and I found this more intoxicating than Plato.

The Secretary, alarmed, spoke a word of warning. 'He's married, you know,' she said in disturbed tones.

I laughed back at her. 'They all are.' It was Circe's answer. I had learned to smoke – Pearls of Egypt by preference. I could hold my own in persiflage and repartee, if not score, and I never even thought of the wives in England any more than did their husbands. Boxes of chocolate came raining in, so did carnations and roses, till my room was like a garden. I learned it all with enthusiasm. I began to appreciate the French proverb, '*Ce n'est que le premier pas qui coûte*' ['It is only the first step that is difficult'] – it is only in France that one could learn that.

'You're not going to Paris with him, Tiny,' the Secretary said to me one day sternly, remembering my predilections for Paris, 'you're not – I won't let you.'

I looked at her – blowing rings from my Egyptian cigarette – I had learned to do that too. 'Why not?' I queried amusedly.

'Because you'll spoil everything if you do,' she said in desperation.

I looked out of the window. There was England across the seas – solid and prejudiced and strong. Not even the sea could blot England out. 'It's all right,' I said quietly, 'I'm not going. I've told him I'm not. After all, we've both of us got to live in England afterwards.'

'But there isn't only him,' she protested ungrammatically. 'There are others now.'

'I hope there'll be lots,' I said with ardour. 'I've only got six weeks more.'

'Tiny, you're different,' she sighed.

'Yes,' I agreed, contemplating the dull vistas of my past. 'I should think I am.' She was silent.

The Staff, flabbergasted, took to humming, 'I was a good little girl till I met you.' But the Secretary and I had a counter effort. 'We don't want to lose you, but we think you ought to go' came in very neatly after visits of from two-to-three hours. One time I was enjoying a prolonged tête-à-tête with a gallant Artillery Major and began to wonder why nobody else was appearing.

'Where is Captain C?' I said suddenly. 'He said he was coming in this afternoon.'

'Oh, I told Marie Henriette not to let anyone else in – that you were engaged,' the Artillery Major said.

I jumped. I knew the possibilities of that and the gallant Artillery Major had no more tête-à-têtes.

Then there was the dancing. Captain B was one day doing his best to persuade me to come to a dance; he was not the first to try. But I had no great desire to dance again. I said 'no' merely because dancing had always bored me.

To my surprise, nobody ever believed that. They thought there was some mystery behind it, and the more I refused, the more keenly I was begged to dance. And Captain B would not take 'no' for an answer.

'Come to the dance anyway,' he pleaded. 'You'll want to dance if you see the others.'

'Come and sit in the corner like a wallflower, no thank you!' I retorted.

'You won't do that – I promise you, you won't do that,' he said eagerly.

By this time I knew I wouldn't either and a sudden thought came to me. 'All right,' I laughed, 'I'll come but I won't dance.'

When I entered the ballroom, during a waltz, nobody but Captain B the Artillery Major knew that I was coming. He sat with me till the waltz ended, while I enjoyed the amazed glances of my friends. After that, the fun was fast and furious. I did not dance, but never a girl in the room had so many partners to talk to. And all of them of the most exciting kind and all of them good dancers. For once in my life – strange to say – I was actually belle of a ball. It was in vain that the chaperone suggested introductions – not one of my partners wanted to dance.

Next day the Secretary spoke to me, 'Tiny, you sat out every dance.'

'Every single one,' I sighed with satisfaction. 'It was most amusing.'

'But not moral, my friend,' she laughed.

'Oh, là, là,' I told her. 'What does that matter in France? I only wanted to know if I could do it.'

In England it was the husbands I felt for when the war widows paired off gaily again. But in France I learned better. My admiration for the wisdom of the War Office in refusing to allow wives in France rose to unprecedented heights. I can still hear the officers' toast at School, 'The wives we've left in England and the hearts we leave in France.' It was rather perturbing, but in most cases it fitted the situation exactly. I shall never believe again – as I did in England – that because a man is married, he will not make love to anybody but his wife. I am afraid I smile at the thought now. And there is one other result too. Since leaving France, I have never been able to read a novel or listen to a play without boredom. They are so slow – dead slow – as the men used to say of the prose of Sir Thomas Browne. And the books make love so badly. I could give them points every time in how to do it well. We managed things better in France.

But in all the whirl of laughter and lovemaking, with its undertone of sadness – for we all knew it couldn't last and that serious life awaited us soon – in it all there was one rope that held. It wasn't what we had been told was right or wrong – nor yet what we believed to be right and wrong. Not a little bit. I was greatly surprised to find that it wasn't. Nothing I ever read or believed would have kept me from going to Paris. No! But in the last resort, the only rope that held was that we mustn't let the home folks down. And on the whole we didn't. Still when the bandmaster proposed to play off the departing transport with 'The Girl I Left Behind Me' on the plea that it was always played when troops were leaving, even the Base Commandant grew hot. With thoughts of an amused France behind him, he suppressed the band, and the troops departed – unplayed! But it isn't the French population that would have been shocked – it was the *Daily Mail*.

I was looking out across the Channel one day as the train ferry came in. 'Wouldn't it be nice,' I said to Captain L who was walking with me, 'if we had a surprise ship from home, bringing all the wives? We'd have them all to tea at School to meet their husbands.'

'Heaven forbid!' he ejaculated fervently. 'What awful things you do think about.'

Many months afterwards Miss Mordaunt met him with his wife in the Strand – a staid, conventional Captain L very different from ours. If I had been there, I should have been tempted to hum:

I love them all just a little bit, just a little bit – that's true
Each little girl is a rare little pearl, but any little girl will do.
Some men love just one girl and some love two or three
But I love them all just a little bit, just a little bit for me.

I wonder if he would have smiled – he had heard it often enough.

It is odd how these jaunty little airs sang themselves into our hearts and heads over there. I was never musical so I learnt to love them all. Play 'If You Were The Only Girl in the World' and I see nothing but a crowded hut and the men all clamouring for tea and Twist. Or 'Blue Eyes, Blue Eyes, Sweetest I Ever Saw' bring back rows of khaki at unforgettable concerts. And when the hours are slow, I have only to hear the barrel organ stammer out 'K-K-K-Katy' to sweep away the years between and see me back in an old French street with the Army on either side.

But there is one song I hope I shall never hear again – 'Roses of Picardy'. These are France and all France – they go with the English bugles blowing over the mud of Martin-Église where the Demob camp was – they go with the streets of Arras as I walked down them one March morning and English voices sang snatches from the windows, 'Roses are blooming in Picardy, But there's never a rose like you'– and they go with Thiepval Wood at three o'clock in the morning and the Battery Major who asked me to marry him there and then.

No – 'Roses of Picardy' are too redolent of France and carry too many memories and too much pain for me.[4]

There's another song too that always brings back demobbing time. Miss Mordaunt was stationed at the big Demob camp a few miles from our Base. She was the only young woman there, as she could keep her head under all circumstances. The canteens – at the CC's urgent request – sent only elderly ladies, for here troops only stayed three days to be washed, fitted out with clean clothes and made respectable for England. It was the wildest three days of their lives. There was nothing they would not say or do; they were clean daft with joy. Many times on a Sunday – our slackest day – I went out to spend the day with Miss Mordaunt. In the village street the men were busy buying 'souvenirs of France' as if four years of it wasn't enough 'souvenir' by itself, but, as we passed, we heard the snatches of the song that we delighted to hear:

> Hullo! Hullo! Hullo! It's an English girl again,
> English eyes, English nose,
> English hair and English clothes.
> Hullo! Hullo! Hullo! to me it's very plain,
> The days of the war are over
> It's an English girl again.

Sometimes they sang it, sometimes they whistled it, sometimes they hummed it, but they wouldn't have been demobbing troops without it. And the officers billeted in the dear old Clos Normand, where Miss Mordaunt and I had lunch – they all of them talked to us, laughed with us, flirted with us with that frank camaraderie that the breaking of all conventions gives.[5] For three days there was no such thing as convention – it was like drinking Monsieur's champagne. But the Lady of the Lovely Hair was unperturbed.

If the British Army – all ranks – was delighted to see English girls again, it was not one whit less pleased to meet little children. 'L'Ami des petits français' printed the current number of *Les Annales*, showing an English Tommy with a crowd of ragged French children round him and a couple of them on his shoulder and in his arms. It was no less than the truth. Out at Martin-Èglise nearly every batch of returning officers wished to celebrate its farewell to France by giving a treat to the village children, but, as the treats would then have occurred at intervals of three days, even the French mothers took alarm for the digestion of their bairns. But treats of a kind there were – clothes and toys and Christmas trees, crackers and fruit and good things of all sorts were showered on '*les petits français*'. If it were possible, the men would have out-done their officers in this.

At the Base I saw even more striking testimony of our troops' love of chil-dren. The *rapatriés* were coming back – they had been four years at Lille, Douai and such places under Boche occupation and were now being shipped back to France from Rotterdam. I was on the pier many times to see their boat come in. Wild-eyed, miserable, ill-clad, with a world of patience – and of horror – in their eyes – they came slowly ashore and some of them kissed the ground as they landed. For it was the ground of France. Some looked old men of eighty, some very old women, and there were middle-aged, and children of all ages.

The *rapatriés* had to walk about half a mile along the sea front to the Casino, where the French Government sheltered and tended them. The boat arrived at all sorts of odd hours. Yet it never arrived once without English soldiers – somehow by chance – being there to meet it and carry up the children from the pier to the Casino. It never seemed to occur to Frenchmen to do anything of the sort. One day, as I was going with a wee French baby in my arms in the procession, we met a lorry load of Boche prisoners going back to their camp. The *rapatriés* were afoot, dispirited, dog-tired – as despairing as human beings can be. The Boche prisoners were well fed, in good condition, in the prime of life. And their lorry went superbly well. But if it had been a Rolls Royce itself it would not have got past the *rapatriés*. For the first time I realised what I had often heard from our officers, 'These French aren't much to look at, but they fight like the devil himself.' The *rapatriés* threw down their bundles, swarmed up on the lorry and in a moment were at the throats of the Boches. A low growl of hate – more like the growl of an animal than of a human being – ran along their lines. It was in vain that the driver of the lorry tried to move, or the French soldiers to protect their prisoners. Stones hurled through the air, curses fell thick and fast, yet the *rapatriés* by and large were long past fighting age – mere human skeletons. The Boches cowered in the lorry and sought in vain for an escape. It was an ugly moment, and if it had not been for our own soldiers, coaxing here, diverting there, I don't know what might have happened. Care was taken that a Boche lorry never again happened to meet *rapatriés*.

And our own men, what of them? How did they strike an Englishwoman, working among them? Base Troops, Demobbing Troops, Remounts, Highlanders, even the Guards – if there is a word in English that describes them better than the Sergeant's 'top-hole', that word they must have. It is universal testimony, but age cannot wither it, nor custom stale! I have heard an officer swear in my presence in France – more than once – but I have never heard a private soldier swear, nor have I ever met the woman who had. I have seen private soldiers drunk and mud-stained and battered after a fight, but I have never seen one rude to a woman.

I sometimes went to serve at a little canteen for dockyard workers – Grangemouth navvies in civil life – in the worst part of the Base at Luneray. The road to it was so bad that for the last half mile no car could get through the mud. Naturally there were no lights, and the road ran past a Chinese labour camp. The district was unsavoury to begin with and, as one stumbled along, to flash the torch on a yellow face almost on one's shoulder, was eerie – and not over safe. After nightfall, no one but the dockers and the Chinese used the road, and only one lady at a time ever went to the canteen. No more could be spared. But nothing untoward ever happened to the Hut Lady going there.

The canteen itself was primitive in the extreme. It was lit only by a few candles as any lamps would be stolen; it served tea in billycans only, as no mugs would remain; its money box was many times ransacked and the thief never discovered; the dockers were filthy, uncouth, often repulsive or even fearsome to look at. But the Hut Lady who went there loved them and refused to leave them, even for a demob camp, and they presented her with the loveliest bouquet of flowers in the Base on Christmas morning. Now and again I took on the canteen for her, and when the time came for me to go down the lonely road – though I left an open counter and a crowded Hut – I never went unnoticed. A docker would slouch up beside me, 'I'll take yer past them Chinks, Miss.' And murderer though he might be in civil life, as I trudged along in the mud beside him, I was as safe as the Bank of England and I knew it.

'Weren't you afraid?' the Chief questioned me once on my return.

'With the British Army all round me?' I rallied him laughingly. 'How could I be safer?' I had learned something from my visits to Luneray.

At the canteen counter, too, I made many friends. 'Goin' on leave tomorrow, Miss,' said one as I gave him a mug of tea. 'Thinkin' o' getting married, Miss, I am,' he volunteered next.

'And a very good thing too,' I agreed warmly.

'Well, I dunno, Miss,' he pondered, 'You see, it's this way. Me and my ole mother lives together rare and comferable-like, we do. An' the chaps do say as 'ow yer wife never tikes the same care o' yer as wot yer ole mother does.'

'An' that's no more than the truth, Bill, no more it ain't. Two teas, Miss, if you please,' interrupted a neighbour, coming up.

The prospective bridegroom looked disturbed. 'But yer carn't 'ave yer ole mother with yer always,' he protested, not unnaturally.

'Then yer best by yerself, Bill: wives is no good nohow,' returned the misogynist, taking a deep draught of tea.

I intervened. 'But the wife might learn from your mother,' I suggested rashly. The despairing one finished his tea.

'Yer dunno, Miss,' he said, putting the mug down with a thump. 'Yer means well, but yer dunno' – which, indeed, was true. 'Wives never learns,' he added gloomily. But a queue was waiting and they drifted from the counter.

As for ourselves, if the officers were mixed, so were we, and no one was quicker than the soldier to pick out the real from the sham in the lady behind the counter. It was disconcerting how soon he knew, and how ill at ease he felt with the sham. But if he liked you, he took you into his confidence about his inmost domestic life. There were the photographs of course. He always showed you these, producing them from his pay book with pride and reverence. There is a sameness in photographs so shown, but I rapidly chose one child from each group and concentrated on that. 'This is the one I like best,' I said diplomatically, knowing I could not remember them all. 'How old is he?'

At School I saw them in a different light. I think it was their patience in sticking to work they had chosen that I admired most. It was in English only that they had any criterion of dullness or the reverse. In other subjects nothing daunted them.

'Don't you find this boring?' I said to a man who never could get past the first declension in Greek.

He stared at me. 'Oh no, Miss,' he said in wonderment.

I came to the conclusion that one of two things was the reason. Either they expected very little from a foreign language or they had been doing so many dull things within the last four years that their sense of interest was blunted. But if they had inexhaustible patience, they were also many of them incredibly stupid. I hate to use the word 'stupid' for it implies a reproach, and that is the last thing I wish to convey. I mean that they found learning immeasurably hard. And finding it so, they stuck to it. I'm afraid that at home I have no use for the stupid child or the stupid student, but in France the stupidity was so unfathomable and the patience so amazing that I grew fascinated. Had I found Greek as hard as they did, I should never in this world have learnt it. In the end, the stupidest people from all the classes were handed over to me. There was a military policeman who was trying to learn French. Despite many months' teaching, he could not master the form of the French imperfect. He was a policeman in civil life too, with a most Olympian air, and never have I felt so like a criminal, as when I sat down beside him to explain the imperfect. He was huge and I was small – I felt we could have sat for *Dignity and Impudence*.[6] But his mind was quite impenetrable and he never knew when he was beaten. To my amazement he actually signed on for another year in France 'to perfect his French'. He thought he was improving. Some day I shall meet him at a London crossing and I'll ask him the third singular of a French imperfect verb and he will answer wrong.

If the men were stupid, the officers were not much better. I had a Cambridge man for German once. The Secretary was in the room during the lesson and she said to me afterwards, 'He's not clever, is he?'

'No,' I returned. 'Stupid as they make them.'

'I thought that,' she heaved a sigh of relief. 'But he was at Cambridge?'

'Ah well, he's been in the Army since.'

But he wanted a German lesson every single day and he wanted it all by himself. Most of the officers did that. It never was convenient for two of them to come together even if they were at the same stage and worked at the same books. I had a regular court of RTOs from all the Area for German, and all came separately. Most useful friends they were. One time a very ungainly, red-headed Corporal on a motor bicycle presented himself and asked me for a German lesson. Thinking he was the usual type, I took him in and set out the books. But there was a twinkle in his eye.

'You were up for the last May week, weren't you?' he said quietly – not at all as he had spoken before.

I jumped. 'May week?' I stammered.

'I was at Queens' myself – I knew you by sight at Newnham.'

He was clever, was the red-headed Corporal, and our German lessons were a joy. But they sent him up to Cologne – too soon.

What did the men think of it all – of England and of France? I asked them once to write an essay on what they thought of England. These were mostly men who, at home, spend half their lives threatening to strike. But the essays, though ill-expressed, sounded one note with the utmost clearness. There was no country in the world like England. It was not her villages or her Government or the white cliffs of Dover that they wrote of – not they. And they put no superlatives at all. But they chose out two points, in the main, on which she was unquestionably and indubitably ahead of all other nations and most particularly of France. These were – not what you might have thought – her railways and her sanitation. Of the first they appeared to think that French people travelled either in lace-upholstered carriages or in cattle trucks – both bad for different reasons – and that in either case, they put by preference a goods train on in front to keep down the speed. And they one and all objected to 'E-tatt', as they called it, being written everywhere. Why couldn't they have something sensible, like L&NW?

As for sanitation, they stated briefly, France had none.

'France is, was, and always will be a second-rate country,' began one essay, with downright emphasis, and it was what they all thought. There was one thing they mentioned as particularly bad in France – not a thing that a Frenchman would think of – France's cruelty to animals. Scarcely one essay left that out.

But if, in most cases, the men were stupid in learning, they were thoughtful beyond measure in their care of us. If, on a dark night, I was later than usual in leaving School, I need not be alarmed. If an officer was not escorting me, one or two of the men who had just left, would slip out of the darkness to take me safely home. They had been waiting to see that I did not go alone.

Of all the troops I ever taught, the Scotch troops were the cleverest. I was proud of my Glasgow Highlanders and of their volleys of questions. But I was not alone in my pride. The Chief of another Base came to see me one day. He was an Englishman too. 'I wish you would come through and see us,' he said to me. 'We have the Argyll & Sutherlands with us. There isn't a battalion in France to touch them for Education.' One up for Scotland.

And again, if I was visiting a camp, however rough, no matter when I went, early or late, they never failed to present me with a cup of tea. When they knew I was coming, the tea was nicely served and biscuits with it, but I have drunk tea out of a tin mug in a little Hut kitchen with nothing in it but wooden boxes. However raw the troops, they always thought of tea.

One more story and I have done. It was one Sunday morning at Varengeville, a hamlet on the very fringe of our Area. I had walked there with some French people and we went into the only inn in the place for our midday meal. No English troops were camping there, but I heard English voices as I went in. One was raised in song – cheerful but uproarious. In the parlour of the inn stood *Monsieur* and *Madame*, their children, the *bonne* and several of their neighbours, laughing at and trying to eject a very drunk soldier who was endeavouring to persuade them to dance, and incidentally to give himself more wine. A comrade, less drunk, supported his endeavours. It was some minutes after my entrance before they caught sight of me. My French friends, amused too, sat down on the wooden bench beside me. At length, in the rather scornful hilarity, the drunk soldier realised that fresh company had come in. He turned and saw – my uniform. In a moment his song ceased. His face, I saw, was cut and bruised, as if he had been fighting or fallen. But he wore the Mons Star ribbon. There was a general hush of expectancy to see what he would do next. He swayed unsteadily on his feet, but his eyes were steady enough on my uniform. He stumbled up to me. The eyes of all the room were on us now – curious, half-contemptuous eyes. He saluted.

'Beg pardon, Miss – I didn' see as 'ow you were there.'

'That's all right,' I said cheerily getting up. 'You were at Mons weren't you?'

He paused. He seemed to be weighing something in his mind. At last he got it out. 'Will yer shake 'ands, Miss?' He proffered a very dirty hand.

'Shake hands, rather,' I said quickly, 'with a Mons man.'

'I'm not quite myself just now, Miss – 'ad a drop too much, I've 'ad, but I'll go out and not be a'disturbin' of you, Miss.'

''E bin just out o' the shatoo, Miss,' said his comrade, apologetically, as they peaceably left the inn.

The French audience was no longer smiling. They had seen that, drunk as he was, he rated an Englishwoman so much above the French that he would not willingly let her hear or see one unseemly thing. 'They think you're made of gold,' said the Frenchman I was with, wonderingly.

I laughed. 'That's because they're made of gold.'

Human nature is an odd thing. I used to think I was a good judge of it. Anybody can think that in England, where people live so much by convention. But human nature is not conventional. I am a very poor judge of it – I know now – but at least I know this: a man may drink and steal and swear and lie – and yet none of these things will prevent him from being 'a verray parfit gentil knight' to a woman who expects it of him. And he may do none of these things and keep all the conventions that even England honours, and yet be wholly unreliable. With 'other ranks' any of them, drunk or sober, I would go without a qualm down the loneliest road, past the most terrifying Chinese, but if my escort were an officer, I should want to know him first. It is for others to speak of how he fights, but when I think of human nature at its best, I think of the English private soldier in France.

Notes

1. Julia and Mildred were both in Paris from December 1918 onwards, working as typists at the Peace Conference.
2. Henry Brooke's secretary was Miss P.M. Woodroffe.
3. 'Give Me A Little Cosy Corner' was a very recent popular song, written in 1918 by Clifford Harris and James W Tate.
4. Throughout this chapter Christina brings to mind a series of popular songs, evoking powerfully the way in which music offered a release from the horrors of war for both troops and civilians. 'I was a Good Little Girl Till I Met

You' is another Harris and Tate song, this time from 1914, while 'We Don't Want to Lose You' (Paul Rubens) became a huge favourite at the start of the war, used to persuade young men to enlist. Some, like 'If You Were the Only Girl in the World' (1916) have since been recorded and re-recorded and have become classics, while others are today more or less forgotten. It is interesting that the song Christina singles out as carrying 'too many memories and too much pain' is 'Roses of Picardy'. Written in 1916, it was widely popular among the troops but became synonymous with the terrible slaughter which took place in the battlefields of Picardy. You can almost picture Christina sitting, pen in hand, humming the tunes as she writes – and, as the music recalls the emotions of the time, slipping from the frivolous fun of flirting with officers to the remembered pain of the reality of loss.

5. The Auberge de Clos Normand at Martin-Èglise, which still exists today, had in peacetime attracted some of the literary and artistic figures who visited Dieppe. Oscar Wilde came here, and Walter Sickert painted the owner of the inn, Victor Lecour.

6. An interesting insight into how Christina saw herself! *Dignity and Impudence* is a painting by Sir Edwin Landseer of a great bloodhound contrasted with a little West Highland terrier.

8

At a base hospital

There was a Base Hospital at the very limit of our Area. It had been the Base for the Somme Battle in '16 and comprised, indeed, four General Hospitals – two Canadian and two English.[1] We had some workers there, and the Chief suggested one day that I might like to go through and visit them. It was a beautiful Saturday morning when I set off in the car. This time it was a good road. Indeed it was one of the English military roads, forming part of the actual lines of communication. The English wires, with their plain, blunt posts, ran along the left side of the road. The French, on more slender posts, ornamented with curious spirals, held the right. I thought the difference was typical of the nations. The English aimed solely at doing its work. The French must have a little ornament to life as well. The road had been one of Napoleon's, so it ran dead straight. I settled myself back in the Ford – running rippingly, with the road a white ribbon up to the horizon – and prepared to enjoy the pleasant morning. Presently I picked out a flag – red, black and yellow – flapping in the breeze. 'Belgian HQ,' said the chauffeur briefly, as we whizzed past. I sniffed daintily. The Belgian other ranks looked none too prepossessing and their officers slouched. A little later, pointing to an undulating patch on the left, 'Fine camp that made,' he said with enthusiasm. 'The Guards were there all August and September.' I sat up – so that was where Miss Mordaunt had spent her wonderful six weeks.

The countryside was flat and appeared to be well tilled, but we never saw a soul in the fields. In fact, I never have in France – except in the little cottage gardens. We were drawing near the Hospital Base itself when the line of communication branched off and we followed a road up a hill – up a high, high hill, until we came to what seemed to be the little town on top. Nearly every camp I had been to was on a hill, but none of them had a view like this. All the winds of heaven blew here – the sea lay green and fair, away down beneath our feet, and at our side nestled the little red-roofed French town, cosily sheltered under the heights. But the English town of huts was larger – four General Hospitals placed together and coping with the Somme battle needed to be of some size. We drove through street after street of long low huts, with their tiny gardens picked out with white stones. Against the brown background, the hospital blue of the men and the scarlet and grey of an occasional nurse, struck a bright note. It was all very still and quiet and haunted. The Base, with its routine and its excitements, seemed humdrum and to belong to another world.

It was right in the centre of the wooden town that we stopped, at a hut called 'Highland Mary', which was flanked on either side by two smaller huts, being respectively the Roman Catholic and the Church of England chapels. 'Highland Mary' was only half full. The convalescents were being sent home as speedily as possible, and the hospitals were closing down. As for our education work, I found little new. The men were hardly fit for study, but they delighted in Shakespeare readings. After a talk with some of them, I slipped out by myself into the Hospital streets.

For the first time since coming to France, I felt as if I were at last treading in the footsteps of the War. Even the *rapatriés* had not brought it as near as this. The long wards were many of them deserted – increasing the feeling of desolation. Yet only a few short months before, the Boche had been within twenty miles, the Hospital was packed up, ready to go at a moment's notice, and the engines in the station below were waiting with full steam up.

A group of nurses were coming towards me. 'Which is the way to the military cemetery?' I asked one of them as she passed.

Instantly she corrected me. 'You want to know where the boys are?' she said quickly, putting it in the way she knew.

They were not far away it seemed. On the edge of the little brown town was an open field, with a forest of crosses of the same brown wood. They were the first I had seen, and I am always glad that it was in such a beautiful place I saw them. Nothing but Stevenson's winds 'austere and pure' and the call of the seagull flying from a land they had known, and the beat of the waves from a sea that washed England too – home sounds, all of them, to the boys who hadn't made back home. No one at all was there as I went down the lines of crosses. The boys slept two in a grave, sharing even in death, as they had shared so magnificently in life – one cross over both, with the double name. The American Army – characteristically – did not share.

After the first moment, a glance down the lines told where our own folks were. I had no feeling that they were really dead. The military lines, the ranks, the officers lying apart – all gave the impression of an Army asleep, but an Army still. That air of solemnity and pomp that somehow rebuffs one in a home cemetery, was absent here. There was nothing that was not natural and human and common to all of us. No smallest child would have been afraid to go to this cemetery. I think it was the absence of tombstones and inscriptions that did most to produce this effect. An inscription makes a person really dead. It is as conclusive as an obituary notice. It is the last word on him. But the last word had not been said over the boys who lay here.

Here they were from all over the world, and ranks, conditions and degrees, from nearly every regiment. In this one thing only they were alike. Wounded in the Somme, they had come here to die. It seemed hard that they should get to the water's edge and yet have no strength to cross it – that they had to die almost within sight of home. The nearness of the sea and of the land that one could almost discern beyond it – these between them made these crosses tragic. In one corner, by themselves, stood rows of other crosses – Maltese crosses – not quite so simple. Under them lay the Boche prisoners captured at the Somme – who had died here too. Boche and American and Briton side by side now.

Slowly I turned away down the long steep road from the hill. Near the foot stood the house where I was staying – it had been used during the war to put up the relatives of the dangerously wounded.[2] How often they must have climbed by this same road to the Hospital – the road of the ambulances, the road of the relatives, the road of the dead. For the road of the living lay over the water. The house was run by our own people – a Hut Lady in charge and two orderlies to help her. Though the house was lower than the Hospitals, it yet overlooked the French town, and my room – a corner one with a great bow window – looked over the roof far out to sea. When the thick blue curtains were drawn at night and I lay abed by candlelight, I began to dream of all the people who had spent days of distress here. The many rooms lay empty, for of course the war was over. A faint sound, growing louder, struck my ears and I stole to the window. Down the steep hillside crept a ladder of light – twinkling headlights and canvas bodies, as the last of all the convoys slipped down to the station. It went very slowly, but I waited till the last light flickered by and the hill was black again. Black now – for always; never again would it know the grim grey trail that day and night for four years had stolen up and down. I should have been glad, I know, that it was so. It was a bad thing well done with. But I was not. It seemed as if the last friend of all was leaving the boys in the field above. As long as English voices came and went and English bugles blew, they could not be as lonely as they were going to be now. I crept back to bed and fell asleep.

'You didn't hear any footsteps last night, did you?' said the Hut Lady to me cheerfully next morning, over breakfast.

'No,' I said with interest, 'Was there anyone?'

'Only a Boche prisoner trying to escape,' she went on, buttering her toast. 'He got into the kitchen, somehow, the orderly says, and wandered about a bit. They're looking for him in the garden now.'

'What!' I cried in alarm, 'A Boche prisoner wandering about near my bedroom?'

'It's all right,' she soothed me. 'I've been up some time and they've ringed him round now. He must be either in the garden or the field next door to it. Ah! There's a shout – they've got him now, I think.'

I hoped so devoutly. While I had been mooning about at my window, watching the ambulances, a Boche had been prowling about, near my room. If I'd only had a gun, I'd have shot him – piecemeal – if I could. So I thought but probably I should have been scared to death of him had I really set eyes on him.

She went to the window. 'He's wounded,' she remarked, 'and they're taking him to hospital.' I lost all further interest in him.

'Would you like,' she suggested later, 'to go to Tanks today? It's a nice walk and they'll send us back in a car.' But I didn't want to see officers here – that side of life went with the Base – not with the Hospital.

'I'm looking for Scotch soldiers,' I told her hesitatingly, 'and I've only the one day. There weren't any in that cemetery I saw, and there must be some somewhere from the Somme.'

'Lots,' she said quietly. 'There's another cemetery down the hill, next door to the French one.'[3]

It was older and smaller and the big *Calvaire* [cross] from the French cemetery towered over it. But the crosses were the same and on some graves flowers had been planted. A soldier caretaker was digging in one corner. I spoke to him. 'You want to see Captain So and So, Miss,' as if I would meet him face to face. 'He is just down here, the officers are all on the outside.' He saluted and left me.

I thought at first they were all Scotch – it seemed like a Highland Brigade – but there were some others. Here was an English Brigadier side by side with a VAD – the only woman there. And here was I, Highland born, like so many of them, standing empty-handed in their midst. Surely I might bring some message from the hills that were theirs and mine! I had no heather and no tartan but it was winter and there were snowdrops in crowds. So I laid some snowdrops by every Highland cross, and by the officers some carnations, and I hoped the turf might lie as light.

'There is some money over,' said the Hut Lady to me later, 'that the relatives gave me for fruit for the wounded. There aren't any wounded now and the money might just as well go in rose trees for your graves. Would you like that?' So rose trees grow on Highland graves nestling down to the English Channel. I hope they'll blossom – red, red roses – for the love that went with them.

'I can't make out what you did on your weekend,' said the Secretary to me with a puzzled air on my return. 'No officers, no RTOs, no Tanks, and the Chief sent you for a holiday. It seems to have been cemeteries all the time.'

'They weren't real cemeteries – not like the kind at home,' I told her, 'and the men in them aren't really dead. Anybody with them will tell you that. Besides,' I finished, 'they were my own people and we're neither of us Highland for nothing.' (The Secretary is a dear, but she is only English.)

Notes

1. Christina is describing the military hospital complex at Le Tréport. The luxurious Trianon Hotel was converted into a hospital, and numerous tents and huts were erected in the surrounding grounds.

2. The provision of hostels like this was one of the most significant yet little-remembered services provided by the YMCA during the war. Relatives of the dangerously wounded were able to visit their loved ones free of charge.

3. These directions would take Christina to the original military cemetery at Le Tréport, beside the civilian cemetery, and here she would find her 'Scotch soldiers'. The cemetery she had visited on the previous day was Mount Huon Cemetery, which lies high on the cliff tops. It was created beside the military hospital as the original cemetery could no longer cope with the vast numbers of deaths taking place here.

1 Christina as a baby, 1889.

2 Keith family group, c. 1905. William, Louise, Barrogill and Christina are standing. Katie and Peter are seated. Patricia is leaning against her mother, while Mildred sits on the floor and Julia on a chair. Edward has not yet been born.

3 Christina's graduation.

4 The School in Dieppe. 'In happier days an artist from Paris had built it for himself, with its wide windows looking far across the English Channel and its red roof snugly sheltered by warm wooden gables.' (Cadbury Research Library: Special Collections, University of Birmingham YMCA/K/8/1/112)

5 Sub-directors of Education at Dieppe, 4 February 1919. Sir Graham Balfour is seated third from the left. Henry Brooke, Christina's 'Chief', is second from the right in the back row. (Cadbury Research Library: Special Collections, University of Birmingham YMCA/ACC15 F1/7/4)

6 Hotel for relatives of the wounded, Le Tréport. 'Near the foot stood the house where I was staying – it had been used during the war to put up the relatives of the dangerously wounded.' (Cadbury Research Library: Special Collections, University of Birmingham YMCA/K/8/1/92)

7 General Headquarters, Dieppe. 'I was installed in a beautiful big room on the first floor, directly opposite the Education Chief himself. My room possessed two windows facing the sea and a large stove.' (Cadbury Research Library: Special Collections, University of Birmingham YMCA/K/8/1/93)

8 Arras railway station. 'There was not much left of Arras Station, which apparently had had a direct hit.' (Cadbury Research Library: Special Collections, University of Birmingham YMCA/K/8/1/254)

9 Arras. 'The houses were broken, of course – in some a wall had been torn sheer away and we looked into the privacy of every room, standing just as its owner had left it. Broken homes – but not deserted.' (Cadbury Research Library: Special Collections, University of Birmingham YMCA/K/8/1/318)

POST OFFICE TELEGRAPHS.

Office Stamp.

If the Receiver of an Inland Telegram doubts its accuracy, he may have it repeated on payment of half the amount originally paid for its transmission, any fraction of 1d. less than ½d. being reckoned as ½d.; and if it be found that there was any inaccuracy, the amount paid for repetition will be refunded. Special conditions are applicable to the repetition of Foreign Telegrams.

Office of Origin and Service Instructions.

London.

Charges to pay   s.   d.

Handed in at 3-30   Received here at 5-24

TO { Miss Louise   Keith British Linen Bank
House   Thurso Cness.

on the 9th Gordon made
the — supreme sacrifice for
Honour & for all he
held dear will write tonight
my loving thoughts are sent
with this

Agnes

Given to me by Capt. Archer, A.E.F.
13th August 1919

10 Telegram informing Christina's sister Louise of the death of Daniel Gordon Campbell. 'My eyes had turned to the horizon again, to the heights that once were St Eloi. Someone I knew lay there, who had been a Canadian, and it was too far for me to go.'

Monument to Canadian Soldiers who fell at Vimy 9th April 1917

11 Photograph of memorial to the Canadian regiments killed at Vimy, sent to Louise. 'The great high cross, with Canada in white letters, stood high on the crest of the ridge. The Hut Lady and I sat in the shadow of the memorial and looked towards St Eloi.'

12 RAMC ambulances collect the wounded from a battlefield.

13 War graves by a railway line. 'May the earth lie light – be light – under the wooden crosses.'

14 The 'grim, grey, ghastly trees' of a deserted battlefield.

15 The remains of a front-line village. 'I could see nothing but ruins, shattered more terribly than any I had yet seen.'

16 The graves of two members of the Chinese Labour Corps. 'A Chinese Labour Corps had just passed over this part and tidied it up.'

17 The statue of the Virgin balanced on top of Albert Cathedral, before it was finally brought down by British shelling. 'The Virgin has fallen, you see,' said the officer sofity beside me.'

18 British troops march into the remains of Cambrai. 'I felt as if there were ghosts beside us, ghosts looking down on us from the gaps in the walls.'

19 Staff of St Hilda's College, Oxford, October 1919, by Bassano. Christina is standing in the back row on the right. This photo was taken just months after her return from France. (© National Portrait Gallery, London)

20 Two sketches from the *Book of the 12th Battalion Scottish Rifles* by David Barrogill Keith. (By permission of Caithness Archives)

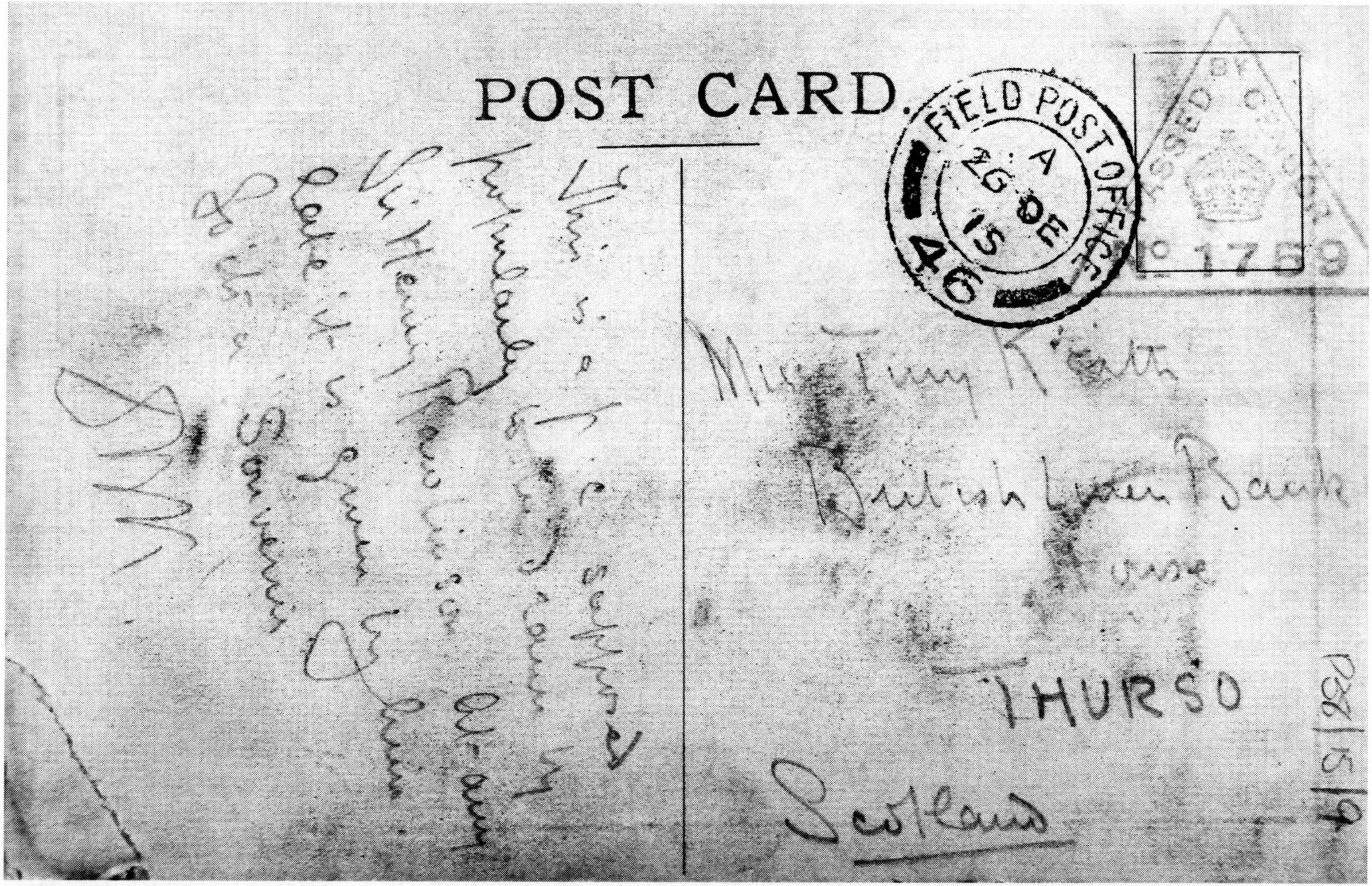

POST CARD.

PASSED BY CENSOR
No 1759

FIELD POST OFFICE
A
26 DE 15
46

This is a pic supposed
popularly to be drawn by
Sir Henry Rawlinson at any
rate it is given by him
so it's a Souvenir

JMcN

Miss Ivy Keith
British Linen Bank
House
THURSO
Scotland

P38/15/9

21 Postcard commemorating the Battle of Loos, sent from Barrogill to Christina, 26 December 1915. (By permission of Caithness Archives)

22 Oil painting of Stromness, Orkney by David Barrogill Keith.

9

Up the line to Amiens – the best days of all

It was the ambition of each one of us to get up the line if we could. We all had red passes, which meant that our movement was restricted and we might not leave the Area in which we were stationed. But if there had been a reason for keeping us there before, there surely was none now. I asked the Chief one day if I could not go. He looked grave. 'You will have to get permission from the APM [Assistant Provost Marshal],' he told me, 'and in any case you cannot go alone. Besides, there's no food up the line. I think you had better wait.'

In sum, that was what all the officers told me. 'You can't possibly do it by rail,' they said. 'Wait a little longer and I'll take you up in my car.' But the longer we waited, the less interesting it would be. I wanted to go at once. Some of our men workers had been up – into the Zone des Armées – for just a day. They had run all sorts of risks to do it. I wanted to go. But I did not know the APM. A good friend of mine, however, did. He was the man who was responsible to the APM for our good conduct.

'Do try him!' I begged. 'He can only say "No" at any rate and he won't be angry with you for asking.'

'Give me your red pass,' he said briefly, 'and I'll see what I can do.'

A few days later he drew me aside. 'I've got a permit for two of you,' he announced, 'as far as Amiens. After that you'll have to wangle it. And, as you're the first to get it, you'll have to be jolly quiet about it.'

Overjoyed I dashed off to the Chief. 'You will have to take a Hut Lady with you,' he said sternly, 'a serious and sensible one too. No! My Secretary won't do.' (In any case she preferred to wait for the promised car. 'I don't believe you'll ever see anything going by rail,' she told me, 'and so uncomfortable too.')

But the officers were good sports. It appeared that the APM's permit did not cover railway travelling. 'He only says you may go there,' explained the RTO over a German lesson. 'He doesn't say how. And I can hold you up on the train. He's got nothing to do with that.'

'Oh, but you wouldn't,' I cried in dismay. 'Do give me that bit of paper that lets me go – you know what it is. Please do let me go.' It was too cruel to be stopped like this.

'You don't know what you're going to,' he said gruffly.

'No,' I coaxed, 'but I'll tell you all about it when I come back. And the most English of all the Hut Ladies is coming with me – you should see her – nothing could happen to me with her.'

'I wish I were going with you,' he laughed.

'So do I,' I sighed. 'I should see everything then.'

The AMLO [Assistant Military Landing Officer] was discouraging. 'I can't imagine what you want to see,' he said, in tones of the utmost surprise, 'and in any case you won't see it.' It sounded final enough.

The Hut Lady was delighted to go, but she impressed on me that I was to do all the wangling. She took no responsibility at all – washed her hands of the whole affair – but she would do as she was told – exactly as she was told. I began to feel frightened, which was rather awkward, seeing I was still determined to go.

'Do you think I'll manage?' I asked the Chief anxiously.

'What about the trains?' he enquired.

'I've got six movement orders from the RTO,' I replied eagerly. 'He said I could fill them in for wherever I want. That's all right isn't it?'

The Chief roared. 'Very much all right,' he laughed. 'With those,' he went on, 'and the APM's permit, I think you should just bring it off. I'd trust you as soon as anyone I know, to wangle it.' This was the only comfort I got and I hung on to it.

At my billet, Madame packed stores of bread and chocolate, tins of bully beef and a few eggs, as we could not reckon on getting any food to buy up the line and of course we would not have our rations. Such hotels, it appears, as were open in Amiens, were crowded to the door with the returning French. At this news, the Hut Lady took pillowslips, as we were prepared now to sleep on our suitcases on the station platform.

The first train we had to catch left at 5 a.m. — it was not prompt, though we were, and I was quarter of an hour at the *guichet* before the ticket office would consent to giving me tickets at all. '*Pas militaire,*' the man kept repeating. '*Impossible, Mlle, pas militaire* [not military].'

But I had not got as far as that to be stopped by a French ticket clerk. The Hut Lady stood impassive by the suitcases. I had an idea. '*Deux billets pour* Eu — *militaire,*' ['Two tickets for Eu — military,'] I demanded, mentioning the first place where I knew we would have to change and at the same time slipping a couple of francs into his hand. It was the only bribe I ever needed to give in France. He gave me the tickets to Eu, and we climbed into the train. Though Eu was only twelve miles off as the crow flies, it was a good three hours' run by the French train, which works on the plan of calling everywhere else first, in the vain hope of eluding its destination if at all possible. Before we got to Eu, I had to think of some plan to persuade the railway authorities that we were '*militaire*' and so make them willing to accept the RTO's order.

A padre, entering at one of the stations, provided the requisite excuse. As padres do, he began to talk to us at once and I forgot my customary code that padres were all 'duds' and told him of our difficulty. 'I'll get the tickets for you,' he said, 'at Eu.' But of course he got the wrong ones — '*civils*' — which made us pay four times as much as if he'd used the RTO's movement order. Padres are duds — I lost this one as soon as we got to Amiens.

It was at Abbeville that we first struck the Somme, and as I leant out of the window, I wondered to see how sluggish and placid was its flow. By its banks, on either side, lay trees hewn to the ground. They had blocked no path, they had done no harm, but there they lay. 'The Boche did that,' said a quiet-looking man in civilian clothes. We were going very slowly now — so slowly that he did a thing I had only read of in fiction before. He got out of the train and collected two shell cases, one for the Hut Lady and one for me and came in again — all without the train stopping.

It was late in the afternoon when at last — beyond my expectation — we pulled up at Amiens. The station was crowded, mostly with French and English soldiers, and I made a beeline for the *sortie* marked 'for English army only'. Amiens lay before us and the mud on her streets was much the same as the mud at our Base. We were rather exhausted with our long journey — about twelve hours now — and sadly in need of a drink, but I knew we must find the RTO before we did anything. It was four o'clock in the afternoon, and we did not know a soul in

Amiens – we had nowhere to go to, and we had not even permission to re-enter the station. Happily the RTO was not far off and I managed actually to see him.

He was in a little wooden room with three other officers when I went in. I must say it was the padre who had found him for me and who had insisted that my one chance of success lay in seeing the RTO himself.

The great man was rather amused – fortunately for me. I knew I wasn't looking wholly unpresentable because my uniform was always smart, and whilst the padre had been burrowing about for the office, I had taken the precaution of smoothing my hair and powdering my nose. Once inside the little wooden room, I found myself deserted. The padre vanished, and the Hut Lady, true to her promise, stood outside with the suitcases. I was alone with four strange officers and nearly all of them with coloured tabs.

'Well, and what can I do for you?' began the RTO as if he were talking to a pet dog.

'Oh, just ever so much' I answered warmly, 'if you'll only be so kind.'

He laughed. 'I suppose I've got to be so kind now,' he murmured. 'Well, out with it.' I told him. 'Devastated areas,' he echoed, with some astonishment. 'I can't think whatever you want to go there for.'

'We've only got four days' leave,' I pleaded. 'It won't take long.'

'I wouldn't go if you paid me,' he said. 'It's much nicer here.'

At this point I was very near using the final weapon in my armoury, which was that I was kith and kin with the 51st Division. And who had a better right to see the ground they'd won? It would be ill on his part to refuse me.' But I thought better of using this dramatic weapon. I looked helpless instead. I could do that very nicely by this time.

A tall officer, lounging in a corner, now spoke up. 'Oh, let her go. It'll be rather fun to hear what she thinks of it.'

The RTO looked at me through his eyeglasses. 'Well,' he said finally, 'if I'm to be so kind, you'll have to be so good.' Not knowing what he was driving at, I thought it better to promise.

'D'you know anything about the way?' said the tall officer.

'No,' I answered, forlornly helpless again.

He drew a sketch plan. 'There,' he said, 'take this with you. These are some of the places you will pass.'

Relieved and thanking them all, I prepared to go. The RTO stopped me. 'By the way,' he said, 'Where are you stopping tonight?'

'I don't know,' I said cheerily, too happy at having got permission to care where I stayed. 'I suppose we'll try some of the Hotels.'

He sat up. 'You jolly well won't,' he said.

'You can't go to the Hotels,' explained the tall officer quietly. Where were we to go then? Was it to be the station platform and the Hut Lady's clean pillowslips after all?

'There's a YMCA Ladies' Hostel,' said the RTO briefly, writing out the address for me. 'It's just five minutes' walk from here. You go to it.'

My heart sank into my boots. Four days' leave and to spend them in a YMCA Ladies' Hostel! How boring it sounded! But I thanked him sweetly and departed.

The Hut Lady was waiting and I told her what had happened. We trudged down in the mud to the hostel – lugging our suitcases – heavy with our provisions. After a long time a '*bonne*' came to the door. No – there was no room in the Hostel, nor wouldn't be – it sounded like England at its worst – no – we couldn't sleep on the hall floor – there wasn't a hall anyway. The door banged. 'I can't go another inch,' said the Hut Lady dejectedly. 'I'm dead beat!' and she sat down on her suitcase in the street.

I was tired myself, but we had to get somewhere to go to. I spied a military policeman at the corner of the street. 'You wait here,' I said. 'I'll go and speak to him.' He was affable and encouraging. There was an Officers' Leave Club right in the middle of town – badly shelled, it had been – but when there was room it sometimes took in VADs. Yes, we could get a cab there. He hailed one. I flew to the Hut Lady. Our luck had turned. 'Other ranks when you're in a corner,' I said to myself. The French cab rumbled down the Grande Rue, past one huge gaping shell hole that had been a bazaar, until we came face to face with the cathedral, sandbagged from top to bottom. We turned sharply off to the left, through any number of small winding streets until I began to despair of ever finding my way back to the station.

At last the cabby pulled up before a gloomy building like a prison. 'It's in there,' he told us quite amiably. We paid him and walked into the courtyard – ankle deep in mud. After a bit we saw a flight of steps leading to what seemed a door in the wall. The windows were few and very high up. Not a person was about in the great courtyard, though there were tracks of recent motors in the mud. We climbed the steps and knocked at the door. To our joy, an English orderly answered promptly. He looked surprised, but delighted to see us. There was a Church Army lady in charge, he told us. We must see her. I was ready to see anybody by this time, but had very slight hopes of the Church Army lady showing favour to us. After all, we had no call on her – as they say at home. She was tall and gracious as she came forward to survey us. 'I have no food,' she said thoughtfully.

'Oh, we have plenty,' I put in eagerly. 'It's only if we could get beds, or if you'd let us sleep on the floor. The RTO said we mustn't go to hotels.'

She brightened at the mention of his name. 'Did the RTO send you here?' she enquired.

'No,' I said rapidly, and as I hoped tactfully, 'he sent us to the nearer place – the YMCA – but there was no room for us there.'

She sniffed. 'There never is.' Then she made up her mind. 'I will take you in,' she said.

I don't think I have ever been more thankful in my life. The place looked like a barracks, but had originally been some kind of a huge store. It had no light and no water, both having been cut off by the shells. She was leading the way upstairs through a large loft which had been made into a most charming sitting room, into a long dark corridor. A row of small rooms opened off it, separated from each other by wooden partitions. She looked at her list. 'I will give you rooms with doors,' she told us, 'the only two that have doors.' The others, it appeared, had sacking roughly nailed up.

In my room stood a bed – and my heart leapt at the sight – with a couple of army blankets and a pillow on it, a table with an enamel basin and ewer on it, a minute looking-glass on the wall and a candlestick. I was overjoyed, and plumped down on my heavy suitcase.

The Church Army lady surveyed me critically. 'You look tired,' she said at length. 'I can't give you any dinner, but if you like, the orderly will give you tea and bread and jam. We have plenty of those.'

Could anything be nicer? When she had gone I climbed on to the bed and simply sat and did nothing. In a minute or so my Hut Lady tapped at the door. 'There aren't any sheets, have you noticed?' she said, in horrified tones. 'And there isn't a chair in the place.'

I laughed. 'No,' I said, 'isn't it jolly? It isn't like England a bit.'

'Not a little bit,' she said ruefully.

There was another tap at the door. 'Come in,' I said in surprise, without getting off the bed. The orderly stood at the door with a steaming tin can in his hands.

'I thort as 'ow yer'd like some 'ot water ter wash, Miss,' he said, dumping down the can. 'An' yer tea'll be ready in about five minutes.'

'Not like England a little bit, is it?' I said softly, when he had gone. We unpacked our provisions and took some of the sandwiches in with us. Tea was set in a small hall – the table-cloth was red-and-white French patterned – but the bread was English Army, white and real; so was the sugar – as the Church Army lady had said, there was heaps of it; the milk was our own, condensed, but never having tasted real milk in France, I had begun to like 'Carnation' best of all; there were scones, home-baked, loads of jam, a brown teapot and flowers on the table. A warm stove purred at my side and there was a soft red cushion in the wicker chair behind my back. Every detail seemed a miracle after the prospect of the streets and the station platform.

After tea the Hut Lady spoke. 'You haven't got any paper from the RTO, have you?' she enquired. 'I don't think they'll let us in to the station without that.'

But I had plenty of courage now. 'I'll go back to him,' I said firmly. 'We don't know the time of the train anyway.'

So we strolled back through the little side streets into the Grande Rue. The light was beginning to fade when we went into the cathderal. There were sand-bags everywhere and wooden scaffolding to protect the windows. It was all very different from the peacetime cathedral. But through the prevailing grey and dun there shot one streak of splendour. The flag of France, in sudden bursts of scarlet, flamed down either side of the aisle in long array, and behind the high altar two hung crossed with the flags of all the Allies massed round them. The effect of the tricolour flaring out from the sombre background wherever one chanced to look, reminded me of nothing so much as of France with her back to the wall.

It was dark when we came out, but a few lights were glimmering from the blackness of the streets. The shops in the Grande Rue interested me — the few, that is, that were open. It was possible to buy coffee and the tiniest kind of little cakes — no sweets, naturally, or chocolate of any kind. Penny bazaars, or what seemed to correspond to them, were there — only the prices were far above a penny. At length, after a good twenty minutes' walk, we found ourselves near the station again and the RTO's office. The little wooden room was locked, so I presented myself at the wicket in front.

'Well, little girl, and what is it?' a pleasant-toned voice from the heights greeted me after a minute or two. I must explain that this mode of address was really habitual with strangers. It was the natural thing to call me, for I am small and helpless-looking, and few, if any, of them, knew my name. When I looked up, I found what ought to have been Captain Bairnsfather's Old Bill surveying me with a placid and expressionless stare.[2] It was the quaintest face, with an odd Spanish look about the eyes. It went, too, with the frank unconventionality of address — though I had learnt alas! that went with most things.

'It's about the trains,' I ventured. 'The RTO said we could go up the line.'

'Where?' he questioned.

'To Cambrai,' I said boldly, mentioning the extreme point to which the rail-way then went.

'There's nothing to see there,' he pointed out blandly. 'Who said you might go?'

'A man with blue tabs,' I said in desperation, 'blue all over.' He seemed puzzled. 'He was a big man,' I explained, with patience, 'with the blue here – ' I pointed to my shoulders, '– and blue there, and lots of blue and red …'

'Yes, yes,' he interrupted hastily. 'But you'd much better go to Roisel, you know. There's nothing to see at Cambrai.' I looked blank. 'There are two officers going to Roisel tomorrow by the 8 a.m. train,' he said with determination. 'I'll tell them to look after you. Corporal, make out two passes for these ladies to Roisel.'

'Oh thank you,' I murmured through the wicket, 'and what do we see there?'

'Devastation – lots of it,' he replied tersely. 'That's what you want, isn't it?'

Old Bill's eyes met mine – his were blank and fathomless. I returned his gaze. 'That's what I want,' I said gravely, after a minute.

In the darkening, down the long Grande Rue and through the twisting side streets, we made our way back to the officers' hostel. The officers were at dinner. In the empty sitting room, I studied the map on the wall – it was the first one I had been able to see in France as the shops were forbidden to sell maps of war areas. Yes – tomorrow we would penetrate deep into the heart of the devastated zone. I turned away with a sigh – bed seemed very good. The orderly, with perspiring brow and an array of plates, was bustling through the sitting room. He stopped by me. 'If you gives me your 'ot water bottle, Miss, – I sees it in yer room – I could give you some 'ot water when it comes to washin' up.'

'Oh, could you really?' I said in relieved surprise. 'I'm going to bed straight away, you know.' I felt too sleepy to stand. Never before had I thought it would be possible for me to sleep without a bottle. This indeed was bliss.

'That's all right, Miss,' he went on. 'I'll knock at the door and leave it, when it's ready.'

The window in my little room was so high up that I could see nothing but a few chimneys and the sky. But I looked longingly at the warm grey Army blankets – that were minus sheets. The clean white English pillowcase daintily laid over the ample pillow, reminded me of my country even more effectively than her orderly did. And tomorrow, oh! tomorrow, I thought, as I laid my tired body with rapture on my bed, tomorrow I shall see where my brothers have been and all the things they've never told me of these weary years.

There was a sharp rap at the door, and I had my bottle. I remember thinking, as I fell asleep, that sheets were a mistake.

Notes

1. The 51st (Highland) Division served with distinction in the major battles of the Somme, Arras and Cambrai. Many Caithness men served as part of this division, particularly in the 5th Seaforth Highlanders, the territorial battalion of Caithness and Sutherland. No doubt Christina had particular friends and relatives from home in mind. Her brothers were not part of the 51st (Highland) Division – Barrogill was in the Scottish Rifles, William in the Navy, and Edward was too young to serve.

2. Captain Bairnsfather (1887–1959), a British cartoonist, created the character of 'Old Bill', a British soldier in the trenches. The cartoons were published in the popular weekly magazine *The Bystander*.

10

The forward areas and Cambrai

It was quite dark next morning when I became aware of a persistent and violent knocking at my door. The orderly was used to rousing officers of the British Army, and with the patience acquired in that art, was proceeding to arouse me. After a minute or so, I realised what he was saying. 'Six o'clock, Miss, an' 'ere's your 'ot water,' and then he began again. I felt that I should associate him with hot water and with six o'clock till my dying day – but it was effective. I got up and cheerfully told him so – otherwise, though he would not have come in, he would have continued to chant.

Once up I began to feel excited. This was the Day. But, first I had to dress. All went well till it came to doing my hair. Then, I stood on my suitcase and endeavoured to get my head within range of the small, square glass. But then the candle would not shine on the glass. And it is impossible to do one's hair with one hand and hold the candle with the other. So I gave it up and using both hands I did my hair, as the children say, from memory. Then I collected our provisions – eggs and chocolates and bread – which were to do us for the day – and went down to breakfast.

'Did you sleep at all?' said the Hut Lady plaintively. 'I couldn't – not without sheets.'

'Like a top,' I said firmly. 'Oh, what a nice breakfast.' It was being served by candlelight at a plain wooden table. There was more white bread – English and lots of it – jam and butter, and bacon and a real brown teapot. So English was it all that I looked involuntarily for someone with a newspaper on the opposite side. And sure enough, behind the *Daily Mail*, there sat an officer calmly and stolidly partaking of his breakfast. He lowered the *Mail*, however, at our approach – a tribute which France never failed to wring from the British Army.

The Hut Lady poured out her tea. 'Really, Tiny,' she said unexpectedly, 'you do your hair very much better when there's no glass than when there is.' I shall not add here the Army brother's remarks about its condition 'when there is'.

The officer was not very communicative, but when we rose to go he turned to me. 'Going up the line, aren't you?' he said, as if he knew all about it. 'I will see you on the train.'

It was still dark when we left the Rest Club – the Hut Lady with the bread under her arm, I with the rest of our provisions in a parcel. We also carried our trench coats, in case we had to sleep in them. Not a soul seemed to be astir. Through the many by-streets we found our way easily enough to the cathedral, but which of the many streets from there led to the station, puzzled us. With the aid of a candle and match, we endeavoured to read the names of the streets, so as to find one familiar. It was in vain. The candlelight would not reach to the name. The candle flickered and went out. Eventually we chose one and after many minutes, came upon a solitary pedestrian – rather like a nightbird. 'Oh, but we were much out of the way! Back, back!' he waved us. 'Back to the cathedral.' And he vanished down an alley. Anxiously we retraced our steps until the vast form of the cathedral loomed again before us. I looked at my watch. It was very nearly half past seven and our train – the only one – left at eight. We had been warned to be there early.

Round and round the cathedral we went, looking for landmarks or a guide. Neither was forthcoming. As last, down one of the side streets, I spied a man and woman hurrying along, the man carrying a suitcase. I called to them, but they either did not hear, or at any rate did not answer. In a moment they would be out of sight.

'Come along,' I said to the Hut Lady, 'let's run after them.'

'Heavens! What on earth for?' she enquired naturally enough, but I was already running and she followed. Presently we were within shouting distance. They were rapidly threading their way round corner after corner, avoiding the main streets and chattering rapidly and anxiously to each other. It appeared to concern them little or nothing that they were being hotly pursued by a pair of shouting foreigners, for they never once turned their heads in our direction.

At last I gasped out, '*S'il vous plâit, monsieur, où est la gare?*' ['Please, monsieur, where is the station?']

'*Suivez, suivez toujours,*' ['Follow, keep following'] he called out hurriedly, without turning round, and resumed his conversation with his companion. Anyone watching us would assuredly have considered – and small blame to him – that here were a band of fugitives making their way with all possible speed from the clutches of justice. At last we suddenly turned the corner, and the man in front for the first time turned his head, beckoned with a sweep of the wrist in the opposite direction and then vanished quickly with his companion behind a large block of buildings. The direction of his hand took us to an open square and there beneath us lay the station.

But there was still the dragon at the *guichet* to be braved. I presented the RTO's pass and in a firm voice asked for '*deux premiers militaires à Roisel, s'il vous plâit, monsieur*'. ['two first-class military tickets to Roisel, please, monsieur'.]

Monsieur, from behind the wicket, growled out, '*Pas militaires – civils.*' ['Not military – civilians.']

'*Non, non,*' I retorted sweetly, '*militaires, monsieur. Monsier le RTO l'a dit.*' ['No, no, … military, monsiuer. The Railway Transport Officer said so.']

Monsieur was disposed to argue. The Hut Lady, who had now regained her breath and was standing behind me, called out, 'Oh, never mind the tickets, Tiny. We've only three minutes to catch the train. Come away.' But I am not Scotch for nothing, and I was not going to pay anybody four times as much as I need – which represented the difference between the civil and military ticket. So I whipped out my passport, with its magical '*permis rouge*' enclosed.

'*Regardez, monsieur,*' I began affably, '*nous n'avons que trois minutes pour attraper le train. Mais regardez, c'est écrit ici que nous devons aller.*' ['Look, monsieur, … we have only three minutes to catch the train. And look, it's written here that we must go.'] This was sheer bluff and it was also my last card. He had only to look at the very official-looking '*permis rouge*' to see that nothing of the sort was written there. I suppose I ought to have been ashamed of this statement – as of many another thing I did in France, but then and now I was unable to feel any shame for it. The French 'did' us so thoroughly in most things that I felt quite justified in getting a little of my own back. Also, if the RTO said we were '*militaires*' it was for no petty French official to say we were not. This time he just glanced at the '*permis rouge*', banged out the tickets, and we dashed for the platform.

It was a military train and the guard had already signalled for it to depart. But an English officer was still standing on the platform, with his carriage door open, though the train had begun to move. We were flying past him, when he suddenly caught me by the arm. 'Going up the line aren't you?' he said amicably. 'We thought you were going to lose your train. Here are your seats.'

Almost head first we entered what seemed an already crowded carriage. Someone took my parcel from me, someone else my trench coat, and I realised that my hair was falling in vast confusion over my shoulders. My face must have been peach coloured and my breath was coming in short, quick gasps. I never am any good at running. The Hut Lady opposite me sat immaculate but breathless. My friend who had pushed me into the carriage, was seated beside me – in leisurely fashion inspecting me. Four other officers were doing the same, two languidly and with some amusement in the far corner of the carriage; the two others with more matter-of-fact attention. I had given up apologising for abrupt entrances into railway carriages since I came to France. Nothing else seemed to have been my fate since the days when the Corporal at Rouen had flung me into the Dieppe train. So I endured the stares until my breath came back and then, because I must, took off my hat. The Hut Lady engaged two of the officers in conversation while I hastily, but quite composedly, did my hair.

In a minute the man sitting next to me began to talk; he was an Australian, going to Villers Bretonneux to search for the graves of some of his comrades who had been killed there on 8 August.[1] In my ignorance I had never heard of that special push, when the Boche got his nearest to Amiens. But now – thanks to the slowness of the French train – the details of the battle were pointed out to me at first hand by one who had taken part in it.

At first the land was not so much scarred – this house had been So-and-so's headquarters; here had been a CCS – these trenches were where the Americans, who had been holding part of the line, had let the Australians down and the Boche through.

'The Americans?' I queried with interest. I had met none of them yet. 'Weren't they any good?'

'No damn good at all,' came the answer, curt and deep. 'No discipline and all talk. After they broke here, they had to ask us to lend our officers to stiffen their men. Now they say they've won the war,' he added bitterly. I made a mental note to watch any Americans I might come across to see if this were true. He seemed a fair-minded man, and the man who was talking to the Hut Lady corroborated his statement. By now the houses had begun to get fewer; there was no longer any building that could have served – even temporarily – as a

Headquarters. The land was cut across with trenches and strewn with debris of a massive kind, derelict tanks and wagons. There was no smaller debris – at any rate to be seen from the railway carriage – as a Chinese Labour Corps had just passed over this part and tidied it up.[2] I strained my eyes and memory to just where the Australian lines had been, just where the Americans had let them down, just how far the Boche had got – so that on our way back I might readily recognise them.

Far as the eye could see, the land was desolate – no smoke from any house, no house itself – but so far it did not look unnatural. I was used to barren, bleak spaces bereft of human habitation, and this looked only as if it had been recently used and then suddenly abandoned.[3]

Even the French trains must arrive some time, and this one at last drew up at Villers Bretonneux and the Australian got out. He purposed marching over the battlefield with his map and compass and returning by the evening train. As soon as he was gone, the officer next to me moved up in friendly conversation. I was now seated by the window and he, as it were, sat all round me – completely screening me from the languid officers who conversed in a low tone at the other end of the carriage. I was not embarrassed. Whatever one did seemed natural nowadays in France.

But the landscape was changing now – we were moving slowly towards Péronne. The railway cutting itself had been used as a means of defence or offence – I did not know which. Its cream, chalky sides were honeycombed with dugouts, and with dugouts that seemed to have been abandoned in headlong flight. The first blue-grey overcoat that I saw lying carelessly at the mouth of a dugout, made me start. But it was only one of a series. Overcoats, crumpled dust-grey caps with their red edges, empty shell cases, rifles – all these lined our path. The Boche had left in a hurry and the Chinese Labour Corps had not yet reached so far to tidy up the battlefield. We had passed the Chinese, indeed, soon after Villers Bret, placidly and matter-of-factly clearing up the mess. Their faces were as expressionless as if they were scavenging a High Street.

Now, beyond the railway cutting, there were masses of barbed wire, heaps of ragged green stuff that we were told was 'camouflage' for the artillery, now and then the muzzle of a gun sticking out of the battered grey ground. An occasional heap of stones marked where I suppose a house had once stood, an occasional stump recalled a tree. Sometimes, in the middle distance, often nearer at hand, the eye lighted gratefully on a few irregular crosses in little groups together. Now and then a solitary one – simple or Maltese – stood by the cutting itself.

It was with a shock of surprise that I came gradually to recognise how the eye did lighten with relief as it fell upon these crosses. At the Base, where they stood in rows and looked across the sea to England, nothing had seemed sadder, nothing more poignant. And here they were up the Line itself, coming to the eye like something normal, the one normal thing in this strange world. It was as if weary with looking on earth that was no earth, on grass that was blasted beyond recognition, on ruins that were uncanny in their desolation, on trees that were stark, on silence that was like the depths of a pit, weary of all this, one turned with thankfulness to the only thing that one could recognise, the only thing that was normal or peaceful here. For it was both, in a supreme degree. Never again will I think of Death as frightening or terrific. The panoply he wears in England, the ghastly hearse, the solemn black, the slow music, the portentous train of mourners – these would menace and cow the lightest heart. But Death is not like that. Down 'where the boys are' at Le Tréport, I guessed it was not so: up the line I knew it. Where everything was unnatural and abnormal, the sign of Death alone was simple and kindly. Not even the youngest child would have been afraid of these crosses. It was a strange effect; and yet, when one has lost one's bearings in an uncharted world, it was possibly an effect to be expected.

The officer chattered on by my side – this had happened here, that there. Did I notice the shell holes? That smudge over there had been a hamlet. I listened and I looked – I looked and I listened, but there was nothing here in focus. The Hut Lady on the other side was hearing much the same from her officer. 'Look, Tiny,' she said to me suddenly, 'isn't the sky nice and blue?' It was an odd remark to come from such a prosaic person, but she had obviously been feeling the same oppressiveness as myself. The sky and the crosses were relieving points.

I do not believe the officers beside us felt anything of the sort. They were used to this country. 'Horrible, isn't it?' said one of them indifferently; but long months – perhaps years – of it had made their minds blank to it. Yet even on them it produced a certain effect. It had softened them curiously to even the humblest forms of ordinary life. There were no flowers anywhere, of course, at the moment, and no birds at all, but they spoke without repulsion and even with fondness of rats and cats, while their anxiety to meet us, to do us any service in their power was only, on a higher plane, an instance of the same feeling. I recognised even then dimly that it was not the same as the eagerness of the men at the Base to flirt with us. Later I was to see it still more clearly.

They were talking at the moment of how far we should go in this train. 'If you get out at Roisel with us,' said one, 'and there's a car handy, we could take you right down the Hindenburg Line. You could see the *Kadaverfabrik* where the old Boche burnt down his dead for fat, you know. It's just thereabouts. Of course, if you did the thing properly, you'd have to stay all night.'[4]

'Sleep in the Hindenburg Line?' queried the Hut Lady excitedly.

'There's a hut we're just putting up, that you could have,' he went on musingly. 'But you'd have to sleep on the floor.'

Now after the prospect of the station floor at Amiens and the extreme delight of actually getting a bed instead, I was all for bed, so I'm afraid I did not look encouraging. But the Hut Lady was enraptured. 'Oh, Tiny, shall we not stay?' she turned to me. 'I should so love to write home that I'd slept in the Hindenburg Line. Think how romantic it would be – alone on the Battlefield all night.'

I shuddered. 'I should not like it at all,' I said firmly. 'Just think of the morning; no place to wash, no mirror to do your hair and everybody staring at you when you knew you looked a fright. Besides,' I pointed out, 'if you can't sleep without sheets, you certainly couldn't sleep on the floor.'

'I shouldn't mind for one night,' she retorted valiantly, and I don't believe she would have. She has much more spirit and courage in adventure than I have. There were other difficulties also that I foresaw if we remained all night at Roisel – not difficulties of propriety, I hasten to say, for those never worried me in France, but difficulties of personal comfort, which, I felt sure, would worry our hosts as much as ourselves. But we must get back to Amiens by night.

And now very slowly the train crept into Péronne. It was a military train, but it carried a few refugees with their pitiful bundles making their way home. It appeared that already at Péronne some families had come back and were living in the dugouts by the station. On the platform, indeed, there was one child. My eyes travelled past it idly – quite an ordinary French child of about seven or so – when I was roused by a succession of cries from the train itself. 'Oh, I say!' remarked the man beside me excitedly, 'Look! There's a kid. A kid at Péronne.'

The whole train was saying it too. I put my head out of the window. At every carriage my compatriots were doing the same, welcoming, beckoning, shouting – joy and surprise depicted on their usually unemotional features. The refugees embraced one another, chattered and cried and laughed. The child laughed too, in quite a friendly fashion, and waved his hand to the officers.

'Hullo,' said a voice suddenly at my elbow. It was the officer who had breakfasted with us at Amiens. 'D'you see there's a child, there – a child - in Péronne?'

As if I could have helped noticing with all this fuss! 'Yes, I have seen it,' I remarked meekly, but the intended sarcasm passed over his head.

'Looks like old times – war over and all that,' he went on vaguely, 'with a child at Péronne.'

I said nothing. Things were indeed out of focus in this world if the sight of one small French child could bring a whole trainload of war-hardened English soldiers into a state of wild excitement. And yet not one of them seemed to find it in the least extraordinary that this should be so.

'Where are you going to?' the officer went on abruptly.

'We thought of Roisel,' I replied, 'and if there's a car, to go to the Hindenburg Line.'

'Well,' he said, 'if there's not a car, you won't see anything. You had much better go to Cambrai. If you want devastation,' he continued, 'and I take it you do, you'll get it full blast between Roisel and Cambrai. Nobody's been there yet at all to clear up – not even a Boche prisoner. I'd go to Cambrai if I were you,' and he vanished back to his carriage.

'Tiny, what is happening out there?' queried the Hut Lady petulantly. 'Why don't we get on?'

'We will, in a minute,' I replied soothingly, 'when the Army has got over seeing this child. There are several women and even one child now in Péronne.'

She accepted the explanation in silence and resumed her discussion about Roisel and its possibilities. 'Of course if the car is not at Roisel,' my officer agreed, 'there's nothing much that you can see just there, especially if you want to go back that night.'

'I think we'd better,' I said anxiously looking at the Hut Lady. 'It's awfully good of you to ask us to stay, but we've only got two or three days.'

'All right.' The Hut Lady gave in reluctantly. 'I'd love to say I'd slept on a battlefield, with the soldiers there too, and I'll never have such a chance again. Still, you're running this show and if you say Cambrai, Cambrai it is.' Nobody ever looked less like one who aspired to sleep with soldiers on a battlefield than our immaculate Hut Lady, but human nature, I had learned, is an incongruous thing.

The train drew near to Roisel and the two officers got out. They said 'Goodbye' as warmly and reluctantly as if we had known them a lifetime. Our train moved on, and only the two languid officers, just back from home leave, were left with us. They looked at us rather suspiciously and talked – as they had done all along – in low voices to one another. But the Hut Lady and I were quite relieved to have each other to talk to at last. I pulled out my notebook and jotted down a few things I had seen, and began a letter home, heading it, 'After Roisel'. Yet I wrote but a few words, as every now and then we jumped up to look at something on one or other side of the train.

The desolation here was complete and the destruction absolute. Through the open window not a sound broke the silence; there was not a sign of any kind of life anywhere. 'Hell must be like this,' I thought to myself. 'I am sure it must be like this.' And still I had not seen the worst yet.

'I suppose we ought to go as far as Cambrai,' ventured the Hut Lady doubtfully. 'This looks as good desolation as we'll get anywhere.'

It did indeed. 'I'll ask the officer from Amiens,' I replied, 'the next time he comes up.'

'Oh, so you *are* going on to Cambrai,' he remarked, in tones of pleasure as he greeted us at the next stop. 'I'm going there too. I'll see you at the station.'

'Yes,' I agreed hesitatingly, looking round at what I suppose must be called the surrounding country, though it bore not the faintest resemblance to any country I had ever known. 'D'you think,' I began diplomatically after a silence, 'that perhaps we could get out and walk a bit?'

He stared at me. 'Here do you mean?'

I nodded.

'Good Lord, no!' came the swift reply. 'I do *not* think so.'

I retired, rebuffed, and he went back to his carriage.

But our languid friends were waking up. One of them summoned up courage to address me. 'Are you travelling all by yourselves?' he enquired.

It was my turn to be amazed. 'Why, yes,' I answered, blankly enough.

'Oh, we thought you were with those people who got out at Roisel,' he explained, as an explanation seemed expected.

'Oh, d'you mean because they sat with their arms all round us?' I asked amiably. 'Because I don't even know their names.'

He flushed a little – perhaps not unwarrantably – and the Hut Lady hastily broke in. Her unassailable propriety must have reassured him; and presently they were talking to us in quite friendly fashion, pointing out this landmark and that in the wilderness outside the window. As we drew nearer Cambrai, leaving Gouzeaucourt behind us, every inch almost seemed to have its story to tell. But it was the constant sight of gaping shell holes choked with filthy water, of abandoned tanks, of wrecked lorries and of pitted ground that remained most clearly with me. After the moment, it mattered little to me that this or that had happened at a particular spot. Yet one thing stands out in my memory. Just before we came to Cambrai, one of the officers pointed out what seemed like a deep smudge on the horizon. 'That is Bourlon Wood,' he said briefly. 'You have probably heard of that.' Even now I can see its grim blackness flickering in the distance. Will the day ever come, I wonder, when I shall walk in Bourlon Wood?[5]

It was about one o'clock when we reached Cambrai. We had just grasped our parcels to leave the carriage when the officer who had first spoken to us invited us, in rather embarrassed fashion, to lunch with them at the Officers' Leave Club. We explained we had brought food with us, but our excuses, half-hearted anyway, were soon overruled. Just then the Amiens officer dashed up with the same invitation and I had regretfully to tell him we were already dining there. Once our two new friends had taken us up, they proved themselves most perfect hosts. If ever their eyes should light on this, I hope they will see the record of our best and sincerest thanks. One of them – fair-haired and shy – explained that at the club there was nowhere we could wash our hands. The station had been shelled, but if we would wait, he would go and see whether any vestige of a ladies' waiting room remained. We waited, devoutly hoping there would be; just for the moment the thought of England flitted across my mind. Every rule of '*les convenances*' (propriety) was being broken and yet I thought we were all behaving extraordinarily nicely.

It appeared there were the ruins of a waiting room. When we got there, there was no door, only sacking and little enough of that. Of course all the ordinary paraphernalia of a waiting room had long since gone, but the original label 'Dames', strangely enough, had remained through all the vicissitudes that time had brought. We made our way over the debris of stone and lime on the floor. At least we were not overlooked and we were alone.

'This is very nice, Tiny,' said the Hut Lady, with a sigh of content, seating herself on her trench coat over a heap of metal, and extracting a powder puff and a tiny mirror.

'Very,' I agreed and meant it, but I just wished there was a mirror somewhere that I could see my hair in. The Hut Lady's was the size of a postage stamp – and only revealed the tip of her nose. However, we made ourselves as presentable as might be, and returned to our friends.

A French porter was examining the passes and the tickets. He let the officers through and the Hut Lady, without a murmur, but round me he immediately drew a cordon and penned me in with, it seemed, the entire station staff. It was a detail that I carried the Hut Lady's ticket and pass – she was free to go as she pleased. Like a swarm of bees, the officials surrounded me, all speaking at once. Over their heads I saw the cool figures of the Hut Lady and the officers, steadily waiting for me outside the 'pen'. It appeared that our passes were only to Roisel – that was a slight point, but our tickets were only to there too. It was suspicious, indeed most suspicious, I was told.

'How much extra is it to Cambrai?' I enquired quietly. The question seemed to take them aback. What they had expected me to say I do not know, but my explanation that we wanted to see more and so had come further up the line, seemed to them highly unsatisfactory. They grunted and they growled. The Hut Lady looked more and more perturbed, but the officers stood rigid. They intended me to get free. With the British Army in the support trenches, I felt I would not have turned a hair had the entire staff of the Chemin-de-fer du Nord sought to poind [impound] me. At last a sum was named, which I paid, and stepped once more into freedom. Than the French minor railway servant, I can conceive no greater tyrant and no shiftier official.

Now free in Cambrai, we made our way to the Club. It had been the German Officers' Leave Club right through the war until almost the end, and as Cambrai itself had been held by the Boche, very little damage had been done to the town, and none at all to the Club. Our promise to the French to spare their towns wherever possible had profited Cambrai much. The cathedral, true, was damaged in the fighting at the end of the War and was now out of bounds, as the Royal Engineers had not yet inspected the damage done; the chief square seemed to have been battered, but compared with Péronne, and we were told Arras, Cambrai had suffered relatively little.

The first thing I noticed was the direction posts still in German. 'Nach Bapaume', 'Nach Arras', and further instructions how to get to the principal places in the town. 'There is electric light here,' I said in amazement, as we picked our way down one of the streets, and thinking of the candlelight at Amiens.

'Oh, yes,' said my companion quickly. 'The Boche put all that in, you know. Very methodical is the Boche, and we've just taken it over.' Yet for all that, the town had a deserted, scared look. Many of the houses were standing empty and abandoned – windows were broken, great gaps yawned here and there. The ring of our foot-steps on the *pavé* seemed to be an intrusion on the silence. I felt as if there were ghosts beside us, ghosts looking down on us from the gaps in the walls.

Suddenly, I stopped with a cry. 'Oh, here is a real glass in a window! Now I can see to do my hair.' It was a relief just to say something trivial. A fair-sized glass was actually standing in an abandoned shop in this practically deserted street, and there and then in the roadway, with the officers gravely criticising and the Hut Lady looking somewhat amusedly on, I did my hair. But I was in dead earnest. 'Now,' I said, when I had finished, and giving a last look to the whole, 'now I can face the RTO. We've got to get our passes back to Amiens, you know.'

The officers stared at me. 'D'you mean to say,' one asked, 'you haven't got your passes back to Amiens?'

I shook my head. 'No. They would only give us the passes away from Amiens. We've got to trust to luck to get back again.'

'Well, upon my word,' said the officer, taking a deep breath, 'you are an optimist. We'd better go and see the RTO at once.'

'Oh, Tiny,' interrupted the Hut Lady, 'need you see the RTO just now? We were going to have lunch, I thought. You're always seeing the RTO,' she ended.

'If I don't see him now, we're stuck here, you know, and things may be very unpleasant too. I'll go and see him now. It won't take long.'

They came with me to his little box and I knocked. Up the shutter ran, and the bewildered face of a Corporal looked out and found – me. He started. 'Yes, Miss, certainly, you shall 'ave a pass,' – in fact he would give me some sort of military order which would send me straight back to Amiens without a ticket. It does not sound complimentary, but it was just what we wanted. With my little bit of paper, I went light-heartedly back to the Club for lunch.

For a moment, as we entered the dining room, I felt that Péronne and the wilderness and Cambrai itself must all have been a bad dream and that I was really back in England. White-aproned, white-capped waitresses moved about the little tables set with their spotless linen and shining cutlery; pretty chintz curtains hung from the windows and from behind some palms in a corner, came the subdued strains of a band. Outside were the broken streets, the shelled cathedral, the deserted houses. But here we were at home.

The fair-haired officer noticed my look of astonishment. 'Good, isn't it?' he said appreciatively. 'But the credit is mostly the Boche's. We did the curtains, of course, and rigged out the waitresses. They look English, anyway, though they don't understand a word of it. But we stepped into all the rest when the Boche stepped out. He did himself well, you know.' After the slatternly checked aprons, and the familiar manner of the French servants, I could not take my eyes off the trim black and white, and the military precision of these pseudo-parlourmaids. Even to the menu cards they handed me, it might have been Piccadilly.

The meal they served was simple – rations, with all the will in the world, can hardly be disguised – but the serving itself was admirable. We talked freely and easily, the officers, the Hut Lady and I – just as if it had been Piccadilly and we had all been introduced in the way that England likes. Neither by word or by sign did any of us show that we did not know the other's name – and that was very English too! Would we not like to go to Arras by road – the fair-haired one asked us – he would find out if there was a car going. It would have been delightful, but there was only a luggage car, piled to the top. There was no room for us. With a sigh we made for the station to catch our train again.

But the French railway officials recognised me. If it was suspicious to come to Cambrai, it was still more suspicious to leave it so soon. They formed a cordon round me. The train puffed slowly at the platform. If I could by this time look helpless and solitary when I wanted, I had also learned the art of rather stupid repetition. '*Je vous assure, monsieur,*' I protested earnestly, voice and gesture aiding me, '*mais, je vous assure*' ('I assure you, *monsieur* ... but, I assure you.') The Hut Lady, unimpeachable even to a French eye, had swept past – ticketless though she was – to her calm seat in the train. The fair-haired officer stood by me, in the offing.

'*C'est la même dame qui est venue la matin,*' ['It is the same woman who came this morning,'] confided one porter to his neighbour.

'*Mais oui,*' I took him up in a pained voice, '*naturellement je suis la meme.*' And then bethinking me, I pointed to the pass the Corporal had given me. '*Regardez, monsieur, c'est écrit ici.*' ['Yes ... of course I'm the same woman ... Look, monsieur, it's written here.']

It was a good move. No French railway official wants to read. At last the cordon parted and I was free. 'And a jolly good wangle too,' whispered the fair-haired Englishman as we ran for the train. And so we left Cambrai – amid the friendly smiles and salutes of the British Army on the platform.

Notes

1. In the spring of 1918, during the German offensive, the proximity of Villers Bretonneux to the city of Amiens gave it a particular significance. The Australians recaptured the village from the Germans on 25 April at the cost of many lives. The date which Christina here mentions, 8 August, was the first day of the Battle of Amiens, in which the Allied forces launched a fierce surprise offensive which would ultimately lead to the end of the war. The military cemetery at Villers Bretonneux includes many Australian graves, and the Australian National War Memorial for France is nearby.

2. The Chinese Labour Corps played an important role during the First World War. Around 100,000 Chinese men were recruited by the British Army, particularly from Shandong Province, for non-combat roles in support of the troops. When the war was over many of these were employed in clearing the battlefields.

3. A startling comparison between the empty Caithness moorlands and the devastated battlefield wastelands!

4. The officer is repeating one of the most notorious examples of atrocity propaganda perpetrated by the British press during the First World War. Neither

he nor Christina appears to question the truth of the rumour, although in a letter from 1918 Barrogill also refers to this 'yarn' as something of which the British should be ashamed. Reports of a German factory which boiled down the corpses of its own soldiers for fat appeared in Lord Northcliffe's newspapers *The Times* and the *Daily Mail* in April 1917, apparently based on an article in a Belgian newspaper. The story was widely believed and repeated both at home and among soldiers in the trenches. A complete repudiation was issued by the British government in 1925, but by this time it had contributed significantly to post-war attitudes to Germany. Realisation that the story had been completely untrue also may have contributed to reluctance to believe initial reports of the Holocaust. ['Media and Propaganda: The Northcliffe Press and the Corpse Factory Story of World War 1', Neander & Marlin, *Global Media Journal*, vol. 3, 2010]

5. The Allied attack and German counter-attack which took place in the Cambrai area in November and December 1917 cost tens of thousands of lives on both sides. The 51st Highland Division were among those involved in the desperate battle for Bourlon Wood between 23 and 28 November.

11

To Albert, Arras and Vimy

Our adventures were not at an end. At Gouzeaucourt, a large golden-haired lady in the fascinating uniform of the French nurse, was shown into our compartment by an obsequious English officer. She carried a small brown bag. After a few minutes she began to speak. In peacetime, it appeared, she was a *modiste* [milliner] in Paris – would we like her card? – but of course during the war one could not be that, so she had gone to Amiens to nurse. At this point I must have looked interested – for she was the first French nurse I had met. Did she find the training hard? She stared at me. Train! Ah yes, of course, I was English; but no French lady would go inside a hospital to do what an English nurse did. It was not the same at all in France. I must under-stand. She saw the wounded, of course, in her hospital at Amiens. Being a nurse, of course, she was allowed to do that when other people weren't. And *mon Dieu!* Was it not horrible! And the laundry bills! That was really why she was going back to Amiens now, to settle up with that accursed laundry. One needed a fresh blouse every day and her lingerie was, *bien entendu* [of course], of the most elegant – really the laundry drove her to despair during the war.

A propos of lingerie, she opened her small brown bag. I glanced out at the country we were moving through and then at the small brown bag. It contained a beautiful silver-grey gown of stockinette – a material then new – Parisian to its last stitch – and a rose-coloured jumper of the same. These were models. Their prices ran into hundreds of francs. We could see for ourselves, Madame pointed out, that they did not crush in travelling. We could be oh so *élégantes!* even on a battlefield.

The train slowed down – the women of Péronne came slowly out from their dugouts – the women of Péronne! Madame folded away her exquisite garments with a sigh, into the small brown bag. I looked out to see if there was anything that could have been a house once at Péronne.

And so we got back to Amiens and the Officers' Leave Club. Over the map in the big sitting room I traced out our route for the next day to its terminus at Arras. The Australian officer, who had returned, studied it with me. 'You will have to get out at Longueau,' he said abruptly. 'The return train does not stop at Amiens.'

'Oh,' I gasped, 'and how shall I get from there?'

'By another train,' he answered sensibly enough. 'There is only one,' he added, 'and if you don't come by that, I'll come out to Longueau and fetch you myself.' That was friendly, and I felt more reassured. 'That's all right,' he went on, 'if you don't come back by 8 o'clock, I'll come for you.' It was with these words ringing in my ears that I fell asleep soon after.

'Now then, now then, it's 3 o'clock struck – 3 o'clock,' the voice went on, more emphatically, the rhythmic knocks on the door, beating themselves into my head. This time, once awake, I rose gladly. It was to be the most exciting day of all. In the deep darkness the Hut Lady and I stole down to the station. There was no fear this time of losing our way. At the ticket office, a tall burly officer with fur collar pulled almost over his face, stood directly behind me. His enquiries about his luggage – in a French that was not only idiomatic, but that in accent and tone alike bore the cachet of Paris – his enquiries, fluent and prolonged, overbore the ticket man so effectively that with comparatively little difficulty I got my passes. 'Belgian,' I said disgustedly to myself, looking at his khaki uniform, as I rejoined the Hut Lady and we proceeded through the *salle d'attente* (waiting room) to the platform.

The station was pitch dark, but in the *salle d'attente* itself a few faint lights burned. In the flickering darkness I made out the *horizon bleu* of the *poilu*, as in all manner of odd shapes, it carpeted the floor. I lifted my eyes. The benches were filled with them, the tables, the floor. A steady murmur of sound filled the *salle d'attente*. I caught my breath. My thoughts flew back to a picture I had once seen in Luxemburg, *The Eve of Battle* by Meissonier. Just so did the men all lie on the ground, in utter weariness and exhaustion and dream of the conflict on the morrow.[1]

Wearily we picked our way through the sleeping host and came to the utter blackness of a platform. I discerned a train. Slowly we moved from carriage to carriage – more *poilus* asleep, some French civilians – also asleep. At last we found a forlorn-looking carriage quite empty. In a few moments a French peasant woman, reeking of the soil, stumbled up to share it with us. The Hut Lady looked uncomfortable. I realised that from her it was hardly likely we should hear anything about the landscape through which we were to pass. And it would be country well known to our troops – nearly all of it. 'Pass Albert – with her?' I said to myself. 'I'll go down the train again and see if I can't find someone English,' I told the Hut Lady as I got out.

Slowly and carefully, I passed all the carriages in review once more and at last, from the depths of one, I heard cheery English voices in conversation. They were deep in the carriage, and I stood on the step. The carriage appeared to be packed with luggage. 'Have you room for two?' I enquired doubtfully from the darkness.

The effect was electric. A muttered exclamation came from the depths, then a cry, 'Good Lord!' and then two strong hands fell on my shoulders with a 'Where in the world do you come from?'

I laughed. 'We're going to Arras,' I told him. 'Is there room?'

'Lots,' he answered tersely and collected some of the kit. 'Where's the other of you?'

'Along here,' I pointed, retreating.

'Be sure you come back,' he cried anxiously after me. Joyfully, I summoned the Hut Lady and slowly we felt our way down the train again. But the burly form of the officer I had taken to be Belgian blocked our way. He was enormously tall and the collar was pulled up so close around his face that it was quite impossible to see him. Furthermore, he appeared to take no interest in us whatever. I was beginning to be anxious when a little way down a lantern flashed out and a voice called, 'Arras, ahoy.'

'Here they are,' I cried with relief and once more my arm was seized and we were both drawn into the depths of the carriage. The faint light of the lantern revealed a couple of young officers with a vast supply of kit that might well have furnished a regiment encumbering every part of the carriage. We sat on cleared spaces in the middle and in the open doorway I recognised again the bulk of the tall, fur-collared officer.

'Here are your things, sir,' said one of our young friends respectfully while the great one entered and sat down in the corner opposite me. So he was English then, I reflected, and he spoke the best French I had ever heard an Englishman speak. I had flattered myself I always knew a stranger speaking French, but I had not known him.

The train started, and we moved into a countryside as dark as the station itself. The dim light of the lantern was not enough even to let us see each other. The Hut Lady, I knew, sat on the opposite side next to one of the young officers, who engaged her closely in conversation. I sat almost within the embrace of the other, who told me that he had fought over every inch of ground hereabouts, and that he would point it out to me when it grew light enough. They all belonged to a Battery it seemed, and were going to Valenciennes.

The Major in the corner – for so he turned out to be – suddenly broke into the conversation. 'I saw you at the ticket office,' he began, apparently addressing me.

'Yes,' I replied meekly. 'I thought you were a Belgian.'

'Belgian?' he snorted, sitting up in his corner. The two young officers visibly quailed.

'Only because you spoke such beautiful French,' I added hastily – though, of course, Belgians don't, as he knew.

He seemed mollified. 'I was at School at Paris. You spoke not so badly yourself.' This was indeed praise, I felt. 'Can you do the French "r"?' he queried abruptly.

There was intense silence, I noticed, in the compartment, while he spoke. 'No,' I rejoined sadly. 'I can only make a bad shot at it. I've never heard an Englishman do it as beautifully as you.'

'I'm not English,' he snapped, nettled again. Another brick! I sighed. I dared not venture anything more, but he conceded in a few minutes, 'I am Scotch – from Edinburgh.' It was my turn to jump – and I suppose I did. 'Perhaps you'll say you don't believe that either,' he sparred, 'from the way I speak.' He certainly had the most faultless English accent, as we say at home.

'Oh no,' I returned coolly. 'You see, I'm Scotch too.'

He seemed interested but at that moment the train pulled up with a jerk. We were entering Albert. I stood at the window and looked out. The dawn was just breaking in queer, wavering snatches. Gaunt before me loomed the shell of Albert Cathedral.

'The Virgin has fallen, you see,' said the officer softly beside me. 'She fell shortly before the Armistice. That's the road to Bapaume. Goes straight off three maps.'[2]

I looked at it in silence – the long white road to Bapaume. Indeed, there seemed singularly little to say. I could see nothing but ruins, shattered more terribly than any I had yet seen. But the silence was the same – the silence of Péronne and of Cambrai. It was the silence that I suppose there will be on the Day of Judgment, when we all stand at the Bar. At any rate, it made me think of that. Nothing else seemed like it. The grey mist of dawn and the long white road!

I shivered, as I turned back into the carriage. 'Cold, aren't you?' said the young officer considerately. Then his eyes wandered back to the road. 'Topping road, that,' he echoed appreciatively. 'Goes straight off three maps.'

The Major was asleep in his corner, and his two young companions began to talk in whispers, with many a wary glance at him. I noticed that in the streaky light from the windows the guttering light of the lantern looked unearthly. 'I know every inch here,' confided the Hut Lady's friend. 'Achiet-le-Petit, Achiet-le-Grand. We'll pass these,' he said, scanning the map. 'Just think of a railway being up here now.' I sat opposite the Major, as silent as himself, and the subaltern, with his arm half round me, in a cheerful voice told me where we were.

Curious things were moving outside the window, scarred and shapeless things – in hundreds. They suggested faintly something I had seen long ago – what was it? – something that wasn't true, I knew. It was Arthur Rackham's pictures. I sprang to my feet. 'What are these?' I cried in horror. 'Oh, what are these?'

My companion, whose eyes had mainly been on me, took a cursory glance outside. 'Trees!' he said in astonishment. 'That's Thiepval Wood, you know.'[3]

My cry had awakened the Major. 'Thiepval Wood and the dawn,' he said in his curious loud voice. 'The hour when the boys stood to.'[4]

I stood by the window. The train crawled along. I was grateful for the noise it made. Thiepval Wood! Oh! *Mon Dieu!* 'Hell must be like that,' I said softly. 'Yes – Hell must be like that.'

The Major's heavy hand descended on my arm. 'Little Girl,' said the Major deliberately, 'I've fallen in love with you. Will you marry me?'

I looked at him. '*Mais tout de suite, monsieur,*' ['right away, Monsieur,'] I replied at once. I have never answered a proposal half so speedily before or since.

The Major produced his card. 'My battery is at Valenciennes,' he said. 'You had better come there for a fortnight.'

The Hut Lady looked anxiously over at me. Outside the window those grim grey ghastly trees had receded and the dawn had come. In the bitter light the land lay stark before us. Everything had been done to it that could be done. There was nothing new for it to learn. And yet, so does the mind shrink from dwelling on the blank horror of it all, that every time I call up the picture of Thiepval Wood and what had been its trees, I see again the patchy light falling cold and grey and the desolation that rose and overwhelmed me – but not these alone. Automatically there comes back to me the Major's voice – in its unholy incongruity – though, indeed, nothing human seemed unholy then. I have a lurking feeling that I ought to be ashamed of the coincidence of the three – the wood, the dawn and the Major – but, at the time, the Major was a relief.

'I waited till I could see your face,' he explained later, 'before I asked you to marry me.' It seemed a sensible enough precaution, I thought.

I remember little more till the train drew up at Arras, and the young subalterns busied themselves about helping us out, and telling us what to do. The Major had sunk back again in his corner – as it seemed – asleep. After his sudden proposal to me and his taking for granted that I should accompany him forthwith to Valenciennes, he had taken no further part in the conversation.

'I think he is a lunatic and they are in charge of him,' whispered the Hut Lady to me when we found ourselves alone.

'Only shell shock, I think,' I said, guardedly. After all, I had no desire to admit that a man who had proposed to me – even after he had seen my face – must needs be a lunatic.

There was not much left of Arras Station, which apparently had had a direct hit. And worse still, there was no RTO – at least not at first. But in a siding we found him, and his eyes opened wide as they fell on us.

'Go to Vimy?' he answered, 'Why yes, of course. Down the Grande Rue, and the traffic man at the end of it will stop anything that passes and send you to Vimy. Or, if no lorry's going, the ROD [Railway Operating Division] people will take you up on a light engine. Very glad to see you. Good morning.'

It was between eight and nine in the morning when we turned into the Grande Rue. The houses were broken, of course – in some a wall had been torn sheer away and we looked into the privacy of every room, standing just as its owner had left it. Broken homes – but not deserted. We walked slowly and curiously, gazing at everything. Round the first corner, footsteps wheeled – then halted dead at the sight of us. 'Good morning, Miss,' a cheery voice rang out. We were used to that by now, though not to the tones of surprise – but the next moment a head popped out of a gap in the wall on the other side of the street, and another roar, 'Good morning, Miss,' greeted us.

'He has wakened the street,' I laughed to the Hut Lady and indeed he had. The houses seemed alive with English soldiers and undemonstrative though they are at home, they are incredibly otherwise up the line. Cries of 'Welcome, welcome, welcome!' rang in our ears. We looked from left to right in laughing greeting. Then a motor lorry met us. It drew up hard when it came to us: and the eager driver wanted to know if he could take us anywhere. I explained we wanted to go to Vimy and his face fell. 'Down at the end of the street,' he directed us. 'The traffic man will put you right.' Then with a lingering glance he sped away; we were not going his way. In the Grande Rue I met no French people – no doubt there were some, in the marred and broken houses, but they had long since stopped being interested in strangers.

In the fresh morning air, it felt an unreal world. It could not be that those cries of delight, those shouts of welcome, were for us – two very ordinary Englishwomen walking down the street. Nobody had ever been so delighted to see us before – nobody ever would be again, that I knew quite well. Only in France could things happen like this.

'You look like peace, Miss, you do,' said one fervently, as we passed.

At last we came to the traffic man. He stood where four roads meet, at the outskirts of the town. And one road led to Vimy. 'You could go pretty near anywhere else, Miss,' he said doubtfully, when I asked him, 'but there won't be a lorry for Vimy just yet, I'm thinking.'

'Oh, that's all right,' I said cheerily. 'We'll sit here and eat our breakfast first then. We've the whole day, you know.' So we sat down on the ground and pulled out our bread and chocolate and had our breakfast. It was quite pleasant to eat in the open air, with a running entertainment going on all the while. For every two minutes a lorry or car of some description would draw up and be questioned by the traffic man as to where it was going. Each car looked at us with animation and interest, and then, as the traffic man shook his head, moved reluctantly away.

At last there was an excited waving of hands, and the traffic man imperatively summoned us nearer. The car that was to have the honour of taking us to Vimy was an American Red Cross car, with the most uncommunicative driver I had ever struck. He did just say, 'Pleased to take you, Miss,' as we mounted the box beside him.

The traffic man beneath was beaming. 'Come back soon,' he called to us, as the driver engaged the clutch and we bounded forward. The American's eyes were on the horizon with the strained gaze of a pilot scanning a narrow channel.

'You're not going for wounded, are you?' I enquired timidly and somewhat foolishly.

'St Catherine,' he said tersely, turning his eyes for a moment to what seemed a sea of ruins on our left.[5] Our course lay in the midst of such, until we presently came to a stretch with camps on either side. 'Balmoral Camp' took my eye and turned my thoughts to home. Our presence on the box was a source of eager interest to the troops on either side. A wave of the hand, a cheery greeting, a smile and we were past.

Then we came to open country and the road wound upwards. Stretches of barbed wire, gashes in the ground, trails of camouflage, sandbags in heaps, told us where we were. But they were far less noticeable than they had been from the railway. Our eyes commanded a wide stretch of country, sweeping away to the horizon. For miles all around the air was pure and sweet, and the horror of Thiepval seemed far behind. We saw nobody at all and it was hard to realise that so short ago this had been a battlefield for thousands. Only a lonely cross here and there – or a group of crosses – suggested it. I had begun to fear our American had forgotten all about us and was prepared to carry us to the end of the world when all at once, in the centre of the *champaign* [plain] and at its crest, he stopped.

'This is the Ridge,' he said. 'I'm going on to Lens. Goodbye.' Hardly waiting for our thanks, he whizzed off and we were alone.[6]

The silence was unbroken; the land was desolate. Almost afraid to break the quiet, we moved on to the grass, and with a cry of delight, I stooped down and picked a flower. It was the commonest little yellow thing, which grows in unnoticed thousands at home, but I held it reverently and greedily and the Hut Lady looked at it too.

'Isn't it lovely?' she said lingeringly, stroking it petal by petal. To find a flower after all that we had seen, seemed a miracle.

We moved on and picked up bits of shells, bullets, stray bits of camouflage: all the odds and ends left over from the fighting. The Hut Lady, with more energy than I had, was plunging along a trench while I sat thinking on the parapet, when suddenly a voice said courteously at my side, 'Wouldn't you like a cup of tea?'

If I had been a screaming person, I would have screamed then. I merely started violently and looked up. An English officer, in immaculate uniform, looked amusedly down at me. He held out a billy can in one hand. 'Oh, thank you,' I murmured, utterly tongue-tied.

'Sorry there aren't any cups,' he went on, 'but perhaps you will manage with this. My men always make tea just now. It's eleven o'clock, you know.'

The Hut Lady, hearing the sound of voices, appeared from her trench. She saw me and a strange officer each grasping one end of a billy can, as if in the act of plighting our troth. But she was not nearly as taken aback as I was.

'Oh Tiny, how nice,' she cried, scrambling up. 'Is it actually tea?'

It appeared that the officer, with another, and their men were engaged in clearing up the battle area and found the job rather monotonous. They were eager to show us all they could, when we had finished the tea.

'You would like to go down a dugout, wouldn't you?' asked our guide affably. 'I'll take you down one of ours and one of the Boche's. His are far the best, of course.'

We scrambled down into a trench and he led the way. 'Down here,' he pointed. 'Wait till I light the candle and watch out – the steps are rather slippery.' Before us yawned a cavern, with an almost perpendicular staircase of dripping yellowish mud. I decided not to go first. The Hut Lady and the other officer went on, she chattering eagerly all the while. 'Come along,' said my friend, 'it's quite easy.'

Helped and propped at elbow and shoulder, I managed to descend. A couple of bunks, like those in a steamer, confronted me on the right. They were very low roofed, very narrow and completely dark. Only the wavering light of the candle enabled me to see them at all.

'Officers' bunks,' said the guide briefly. I shivered. 'This is a topping big dugout,' said my companion, in tones of admiration. 'It has a passage right through, so that you can get out at the other side,' and he proceeded to indicate a narrow tunnel in complete blackness, down which I saw the bent and disappearing forms of the Hut Lady and her escort. Moreover, the candle was going with them, and in a minute I should see nothing.

'I'm not going there,' I cried out, 'I'm not going there at all.'

My companion looked blank. 'It comes up the other side,' he explained in bewilderment.

'I'm not going,' I repeated, 'oh, please take me up before it gets dark.'

He began to understand I was terrified, and though he was perfectly polite, he could not prevent a broad smile. 'It won't get dark,' he said, comfortingly. 'There's always light from the trench, you know.'

I was already back at the foot of the staircase. The coats left in the bunks no longer interested me, whether they were Boche or British. 'Oh, there are these awful steps yet,' I cried in dismay, as I faced the slithering yellow wall. 'I don't know how you ever summoned up the courage to come down here,' I cried with a despairing wail, as I edged my way up.

'Courage!' he echoed indignantly. 'Do you know this is one of the very finest dugouts and that you'd be jolly lucky to get to it. If you stayed up there, you'd be shelled.'

By this time I was well 'up there' and even as I stumbled in the slippery ooze of the trench, I heaved a sigh of relief. 'It's awful,' I said shortly, and we walked on in silence.[7]

'Come, and I'll show you a big gun emplacement – Boche,' he said, changing the subject, 'and then we'll look at the Canadian memorial.'

My eyes had turned to the horizon again, to the heights that once were St Eloi. Someone I knew lay there, who had been a Canadian, and it was too far for me to go. I could only see the Ridge where he had been killed, and not the place where he lay.[8] I went quietly to the big gun emplacement. It seemed untouched, and even to my inexperienced eyes, of amazing strength.

'We got held up here I don't know how long,' he explained. 'You see how well it is screened and how it commands all this stretch of ground.'

I wandered out in search of souvenirs when a sharp, 'Don't touch that!' rang out. My hands were on a beautiful large shell case – or so I thought – with a bright red mark on it.

'I can't lift it anyhow,' I said regretfully, still fingering it.

He tore my hands away. 'Good God,' he cried in – I suppose – justifiable indignation. 'You're afraid to go down the finest dugout on the Ridge and you play with an unexploded shell. Don't you know what that red mark means?'

'No,' I said meekly, rather afraid of him now.

'That it's dangerous,' he snapped, 'not inspected yet by the Royal Engineers. This place is full of them. We're only just beginning to clear up.' We walked on in silence.

'It must be wonderful to live up here,' I ventured after a little. 'So open, and you see such long distances and there's nobody at all to disturb you.'

'Jolly lonely sometimes,' he returned. 'Would you like to come up for a weekend?'

'Like to come?' I echoed. 'I'd just love it, but we've only got four days. We must go back tomorrow.'

'Put down those things you're carrying,' he said, glancing at my armful of spent bullets, bits of camouflage, bits of shells and flowers. 'No one will touch them here and I'll snap you at the foot of Canada's cross.'

The great high cross, with Canada in white letters, stood high on the crest of the ridge. The bright March sunlight danced on the white letters and picked out with silver the grey cross. The keen March wind blew like the winds of home over all the quiet field. The Hut Lady and I sat in the shadow of the memorial and looked towards St Eloi.[9]

I have never seen the snapshots for, though our officer carefully took our names and addresses down on his map, he forgot to send them. It was quite natural that he should, I reflected afterwards, for, of all things in France, memory is the shortest. When we came down again, I searched for my treasures, but the little heap was gone. The officer, very perturbed, looked puzzled for a moment, and then he recollected. 'Oh, there are Chinks hereabouts, clearing up,' he told me. 'They must have passed this way.' We had seen and heard nothing, but I was getting used by now to people springing out of nowhere on this strange battlefield.

'It's like the *Pilgrim's Progress*,' I said suddenly. 'Remember when Christian climbs the Hill, his burden falls away. I'm not sorry it's gone now.'

The officer stared in some bewilderment. He had not been brought up on the *Pilgrim's Progress*. 'My men will gather you some things instead,' he promised.

'I wish we could stay up here, Tiny,' said the Hut Lady wistfully, 'while it is like this and before the tourists come. It would be such fun to sleep in those dugouts.'

I shivered. First Roisel and then Vimy – for a respectable English lady, the Hut Lady had most extraordinary tastes. 'Now we'll have to be getting back,' I said regretfully. 'I wonder if we can get a car.'

'Oh yes,' said the officer quickly, 'there's sure to be one if you come to the road – that's if you must go.'

'There's only one thing I haven't seen,' I said slowly, as we went down towards the road.

'What's that? We'll show it you,' said my escort eagerly.

'A dead Boche,' I said. 'I suppose you won't show me that?'

'No, I won't,' he said firmly. 'You shouldn't want to see that.'

My eyes strayed to the little lonely cemeteries, in their hundreds, all around us. The men who lay there were so far from Canada and had given up so much. There was the man who lay at St Eloi and who would never see Scotland again. I turned to my escort. 'It's the thing I want to see most,' I said slowly, 'and there's many a woman would tell you that.'

His eyes were uncomprehending. 'Disgusting,' he said. 'Now tell me when you'll come back for a weekend.'

I laughed. We had not long to wait on the road. In a few moments a French motor lorry came rumbling along, and pulled up at the sight of us. We climbed up, bade our friends farewell, and whirled back to Arras. It was the first French driver I had been with, and after some debate, we decided to tip him. We had only once tried to tip an English soldier and the experience had been so devastating that we had never tried again. But when he let us down at Arras Cathedral, I handed him five francs which he accepted without a murmur and indeed as if he had expected more.

The shell of the cathedral still stood, in part, roofless, and with its interior heaped with stones and rubble. But, as a ruin, it seemed much more impressive and beautiful than, I think, it could have done when new. Especially so today, with the sky a vault of deepest blue bending over the grey stone. We clambered over the ruins till we faced the high altar which still stood unbroken. The great gaps torn in the walls by the hurricane of shells, yawned before us like gashes. The whole place was a living accusation against the evil in man. No wonder the

French Government has decided to keep it as it is for a standing witness against the Boche.[10]

We were sitting eating our last scraps of bread and chocolate, when the vivid '*horizon bleu*' struck in between us and the grey, and a small French Corporal with half a dozen of his men, stood before us. They saluted and eyed us curiously. I looked at the row of ribbons on the Corporal's breast. '*Vive l'Angleterre*,' began the Corporal encouragingly. It was his first remark. He was standing directly in front of me with his men grouped around him.

'*Vive la France, monsieur*,' I returned calmly, '*et à bas les Boches*.' ['down with the Boche']

'*Ah! Les sales Boches*,' ['Ah! The filthy Boche,'] he growled, looking round at the ruined cathedral. He was from the South, he told us, from Carcassonne, and all his fighting had been at Verdun; he and his men had got a few days' leave to come up and see the North. They were like strange, shy children – not like grown men at all, I thought. And they had with them the poetry of the South. 'I am glad,' the Corporal told me gravely, 'to meet Mademoiselle here,' – and his gaze wandered round the ruined walls, and rested by the great high altar, in front of which we were. 'It is right that England and France should be together here, and *les sales Boches* without – always without' – his deep notes were like a curse.

I was surprised, indeed, at the fineness of the thought coming from a plain soldier; it seemed to me more like a visionary or a poet to picture England and France together before the altar in the heart of the battle zone! Yet here we were and behind the symbols he had caught the idea. A gang of Boche prisoners were working outside – he had seen them as he came in. The Hut Lady, looking more English than the English themselves, surveyed him suspiciously at this flight of imagination. She poked the stones with her umbrella in the hope, I think, of distracting him, though she said it was to look for souvenirs.

The Corporal produced his notebook. 'If Mademoiselle would write her name and address,' he begged. I did so gravely, and then he motioned to one of his men to ask the same of the Hut Lady.

At last, taking their great dark eyes away from us, they retired silently whence they had come. 'Mark my words,' said the Hut Lady with amusement, 'an impassioned love letter will follow. You haven't done so badly for one day, Tiny, first the Major and now the Corporal.' Sure enough, the letter did come, even more fervent in tone than any I received from my lonely soldiers!

We wandered out of the cathedral and the Hut Lady shook her umbrella at the Boche soldiers labouring in the street. But for myself, I felt no anger as I looked as them: I felt something worse, as if they were, what the Corporal had said, unclean, and as if I ought to draw my skirts aside as I passed them.

The sunlight still held as we made our way along the street. We wished to find the English military cemetery, in the hope of discovering some graves we knew. It appeared there were two cemeteries and we had only time for one. We chose at random and I asked a passing soldier to direct us. He told us minutely and we were not long in arriving. It was the largest cemetery we had seen and its crosses stretched back, row upon row, like a great army. I gazed around in despair. It was hopeless to discover anyone in this host, and we knew only names and regiments. But there was order even here. 'The men are in years, Miss,' said a soldier who was digging there. 'If you know when he died, you'll find him with his year.'

The Hut Lady took one corner and I another and we walked slowly down the line. One or two soldiers, who chanced to be there, tried to help us, but with wonderful tact, quietly slipped away and left us once they had learned the names we sought. They made no attempt to pursue conversation here. I thought I should never come to an end of the long ranks of 1916 – and there were two years still to come. Latterly I glanced only at the date. In this cemetery there were no flowers and nothing green at all. It was just a sea of the sticky tawny mud, with the crosses planted stark in it. Presently, as I bent to read the names and dates, I became aware that my feet were plunging deeper and deeper into the slime. As 1917 and 1918 grew nearer, the crosses rose from pools of yellow water, like miserable shell holes. Some crosses even stuck out slantingly as if the mud had pushed them aside from their usual ramrod straightness. The mud clung like glue: one sank in it almost as in quicksands. The last rows of crosses in this forlorn place were beyond my reach. I was glad to think that others would soon come who would master the mud and water, so that these last ranks might have their visitors too.

We turned back wearily and silently. It felt a dead weight to pull our shoes out of the mud and the road was far away. The crosses lay between us and that. But we reached the town at last and our thought was to make our way back to the station. As we turned into the Grande Rue, the soldier who had directed us, came up.

'Did you find the place all right, Miss?'

I told him we had, but he still lingered. 'If you wouldn't mind, Miss,' he began again humbly, 'I haven't spoken to an English lady for nearly three years, and if you would just come and have a cup of tea at my billet, Miss,' he glanced hesitatingly at us.

'Thank you, we shall be delighted,' I replied quickly, though I am sure the Hut Lady too felt we could hardly walk another step. And since three in the morning we had not been able to rest for a single moment. But our soldier wanted us to see the sights. Had we seen the Grande Place, or the Petite Place, or the wonderful cellars where the French people lived when the shelling was so bad?" We obediently looked at the first two, and then I asked casually if there was a YMCA canteen near. It appeared there was and we begged to be taken there first. Alas! it was only a rough square hall of a place, with a wholly unimaginative padre in charge. He told us before we even spoke to him, that we could get nothing to eat or drink till the counter opened. No – there were no Hut Ladies at Arras – he smiled grimly from his side of the counter; as far as he knew, there were no English ladies in Arras at all.

'Is there an Officers' Club?' I asked with a forlorn hope. There was certainly that. 'Then we will go there,' I said determinedly, making up my mind that not even a Field Marshal should bar me from its cloakroom. Our guide conducted us there, and we found – oh joy! – water and solitude, the two things we craved most. Ten minutes later, as with powdered noses and clean hands, we marched to our private soldier's billet, I felt I could cope with anything.

The billet was on the ground floor of a broken house. It was a small room with a wooden floor and many boxes thereon. We sat each on a box – never was seat so grateful – and the soldier set about lighting a stove in the corner. I did not care how long he took to get tea, provided he let me sit on my box. The Hut Lady – more valiant than I, who am no campaigner – did most of the talking and heard most of the family history of the soldier and much of interest about Arras too. I daresay I must have heard it all too, but I remember nothing now but the stray fact that a Divisional Footlights Company was giving an excellent performance in the theatre that night, and our friend was begging us to stay for it. He assured us we would be the only Englishwomen there – indeed the only women in the theatre and that we would bring the house down. I sigh now to think of what I might once have done, but then all I felt was relief when the Hut Lady announced that we had to get back to Amiens that night.

Tea came in the end and I woke up to see the thinnest bread and butter I had yet seen in France and a tea tray as immaculate and dainty as might be found in an English drawing room. Our host did not drink with us, but looking for snapshots, telling stories, answering the Hut Lady's questions, set us completely at our ease with that marvellous thoughtfulness for others that the English private soldier always had. It was only towards the end of tea – when I was becoming interested again in my surroundings – that his eyes fell on my shoes. He gave a little cry of distress. 'Oh, if only I had thought,' he cried, 'I would have brushed your shoes for you, before you went to the train. But there's hardly time now,' he added regretfully – then brightening, 'unless you'll wait for another train.'

The Hut Lady looked at my shoes too – severely. She had not waded and jumped in the cemetery as I had and you could still see she wore shoes. But up to my knees my feet were embedded in what felt like yellow plaster of Paris. I surveyed them against the box with quite considerable pride. 'I should like to go home like this,' I said. 'Everybody'd know where I'd been then.'

'You'll be dead beat, walking in that,' said the Hut Lady darkly.

I didn't care – our day's work was done and we were going back to Amiens and to bed. I felt that Heaven itself could only be expressed in terms of beds. A bed, moreover, where I could sleep till eight a.m. – if even the Archangel Michael were to waken me before then I should not get up.

Whilst these thoughts passed in my mind, we were on our way to the station, the Hut Lady and our soldier in front, I trudging along behind. At the station I presented our passes to Madame at the guichet. '*Militaire*,' she said, quite civilly, but firmly, '*pas avant minuit*,' and handed them back. I gasped. ['Military, … not before midnight']

'*Mais il y a un train tout de suite*,' ['But there's a train now'] I protested.

'*Mais oui*,' she agreed, but '*militaires*' could not go by it. It required the permission of Monsieur le RTO français. I looked wildly round for him. She pointed out a little wooden hut, with a queue of blue uniforms outside. I dashed across; the train might come at any moment. Monsieur le RTO was busy – he was a fat man, with black eyes and a huge black moustache. He looked somewhat fearsome. A gallery of minor RTOs stood round him and I had boldly placed myself at the head of the queue.

'*S'il vous plaît, monsieur*,' I began falteringly, '*s'il vous plait*,' … and stopped.

'*Eh, bien, mademoiselle*,' he encouraged me.

I handed him our passes, with my finger on the left-hand corner. '*Quelque chose de gentil ici-bas, s'il vous plaît, monsieur*,' [Something kind here, please, monsieur',] I wheedled, for it was a matter of minutes now. '*Qu'est-ce-que c'est?*' [what's this?] he enquired blankly, at the same time scanning the document.

I explained how Madame at the *guichet* had said his signature was necessary. The blue uniforms listened with lively interest; the Staff directed a concentrated stare on me. There was a moment's silence when you could have heard a pin fall. Then the Chief raised his eyes and fixed them on me, '*Vous n'avez pas le droit de l'avoir*,' he told me and my heart sank to my boots, '*et je n'ai pas le droit de le faire, et*,' he added, reaching for an enormous iron stamping machine and thumping it down, '*et je vais le faire!*' ['You don't have any right to this … and I have no right to do this … and I'm going to do it!'] He handed me the passes and smilingly saluted.

I stared – then said, '*Mille remerciments, monsieur; je vous remercie de tout mon coeur.*' ['A thousand thank yous, monsieur, I thank you with all my heart.'] To which he replied, '*A votre service, mlle.*' With a bow and a smile I ran from the hut. Not without quick laughter from the queue of *poilus* and a parting cry of '*Vive l'Angleterre!*'

With many thanks to the English soldier, we whirled into the waiting express. It was crammed full, and passing along the corridor, we found a compartment of American soldiers with only the corner seats taken. They gave us no greeting, made no effort to dispose their kit more comfortably for us, and after about half an hour, neither the Hut Lady nor I could very well keep our eyes open as we sat bolt upright in the centre. During all our sojourn in France this incident stands out as the only instance we ever met with of lack of thoughtfulness to us from soldiers. They were, I repeat, American. Despite our uniforms, the mud on our shoes and the weariness of our attitudes, they let us sit the whole way, while, fresh from Paris leave, they lolled in their corners. At Longueau, where we had to get out, the carriage door would hardly open and when it did, there was a very considerable leap to the ground. But it was a middle-aged Frenchman who came to our aid there. The Americans sat fast and did nothing. And so back to Amiens and our Australian friend, who sauntered up to us at the station and carried our souvenirs home. He was like an old friend now, instead of an acquaintance of a few days. And then to bed, without sheets, in grey Army blankets – the best bed of all!

Next morning, with reluctant faces, we set out for the Base and everyday life again. It was like bidding farewell to a dreamworld, where everything happened after the heart's desire on a background of infinite horror. Never again shall I visit the zone of the Armies, first because to see a land so wronged by the hand of man, shames one to the soul. Indeed, it leaves no soul, but shame.

'I feel as if I ought to apologise to somebody for this country,' said a prosaic-looking English officer uneasily, as we passed Albert. But somehow it demanded an apology to God. For another reason too, I shall not go there again. If human nature had been at its worst, it had also been at its best. Side by side with ruined Péronne, with desolate Arras, with unearthly Thiepval, there walks in my mind the perfect memory of the men we knew there; welcoming English voices, kindly act and generous thought went with us all the days while we were there, without one jarring discord. We were set about with love. And so it comes that even had I the courage to face that land again, I could not bear the strange faces and the natural indifference that I should encounter now, where once I had met perfection. Plodding down to the Lines of Communication I pictured again the open country and the wide horizons of Vimy, and was glad that the boys who came so far, had found such a lovely place to lie in. May the earth lie light – be light – under the wooden crosses.

Yet Life is no respecter of moods – it delights in contrasts. And even as I stood waiting at the junction for Dieppe, with my thoughts far away, the last of all the RTO's Corporals stood before me.

'Excuse me, Miss,' he was saying, 'you've come from up the line, haven't you? And I was thinking, if you wouldn't mind, that I might give a clean to your shoes before you go to the Base.'

'But I can't take them off,' I protested. 'I've nothing else to wear.'

'I'll clean them here,' he volunteered, and sure enough he did, with what seemed to me an entire battalion looking on with interest. It certainly filled in the time while we were waiting for the train, but I was rather sorry all the same. I should have liked the Chief to see how we had come from the Trenches.

It was about two o'clock when the train pulled up slowly at the Base and we set out to lug our suitcases to the billet. But even then our luck held. The Ladies' Car was just returning from its round of the huts, and it held only one lady, who beckoned us excitedly. The steadiest of all our drivers – and at the Base we had a great variety, including one who was known as 'Sudden Death' – gripped our luggage, and we were landed safe and sound at our billet door. In a way I was glad to be back – for here too was a Bed – I thought of it with a capital B now – and the prospect of hours and hours of sleep before me. It was without a care in the world that I laid me down one hour later. But just as it was growing dusk, I was awakened. The Chief had called – our singing class was giving an exhibition at the local theatre – he desired my presence in his box.

Notes

1. The floor and benches of the station waiting room were crammed with French soldiers dressed in their blue uniforms. As she looked at them, Christina was reminded of a painting by Jean-Louis-Ernest Meissonier (1815–91), who painted many military scenes, and was known for his small-scale detail.

2. 'The Virgin has fallen.' The statue of the Virgin Mary atop Albert Cathedral became one of the icons of this stretch of the Front. From 1915 as a result

of German shellfire the statue hung at a precarious angle. The legend developed among British troops that the fall of the Virgin would signify the end of the war, while German troops were said to believe that whoever brought down the statue would lose the war. In spring 1918 the British shelled the cathedral in order to prevent the Germans using the tower as a lookout, and the statue was destroyed.

3. Arthur Rackham's (1867–1939) illustrations for fairy tales and folklore were well known. As Christina looked out on the scarred remains of Thiepval Wood, she was reminded of his twisted and ethereal depictions of trees.

4. Dawn broke over Thiepval Wood on 1 July 1916 and ushered in the single worst day in the history of the British Army. That first day of the Battle of the Somme cost 60,000 casualties, of whom 20,000 were killed. Today the Thiepval Memorial looms over the landscape, inscribed with the names of 72,000 men who died in this area over the course of the war and who have no known grave.

5. Sainte-Catherine lies to the north of the town of Arras. This area lay on the front line and a series of battles was fought around the town, which was very badly damaged.

6. The high ground of Vimy Ridge provided a natural vantage point of great military significance. In April 1917, as part of the wider Battle of Arras, the Canadian Corps succeeded in winning the Ridge from the Germans at the cost of over 10,000 casualties.

7. In Christina's very real fear at descending into the trenches, we see one of the apparent contradictions of her personality. Brave enough to cross the sea and take on the education of the army, brave enough to negotiate her way across the battlefields, her courage failed her at this moment – just as it had when she was asked to sleep in a house alone in the middle of the woods. One obituary, written by a colleague many years later, stated: 'She was the most unusual mixture of courage and timidity: courage in the big things in life, timidity in its trivialities … She herself used to relate that after reading thrillers late into the night (as was her custom) she was "too frightened to cross the passage" to her bedroom.' The inscription on her gravestone in Thurso reads 'I am not afraid'. [St Hilda's College Report 1962–63].

8. As Christina looks towards St Eloi, we have a rare insight into her personal experience of loss and grief during the war years. The soldier in her thoughts is Captain Daniel Gordon Campbell of the Canadian Infantry, who had been engaged to marry her sister Louise. He had grown up near the Keith family, in Halkirk. Like them he attended the Miller Institute and Edinburgh

University, where he excelled both academically and at sport, representing Scotland at the high jump. A lawyer, he had emigrated to Canada, and was serving with a Canadian regiment when he was killed at Vimy Ridge on 9 April 1917. He is buried in the cemetery at Mont St Eloi. Louise was devastated by his death, and kept detailed scrapbooks which include newspaper cuttings about the Canadian action at Vimy, letters of sympathy from friends, and information about his final resting place.

9. Today Vimy Ridge is the site of the breathtaking Canadian National War Memorial, overlooking the landscape on which so many Canadians lost their lives. More than 11,000 names of those whose grave is unknown are inscribed on the walls of this impressive monument, which was unveiled in 1936. However, even while the war was still continuing, memorials were erected on Vimy Ridge to commemorate the devastating losses suffered by the Canadian troops. Christina and her friend were photographed at the foot of one of these memorials. Louise's scrapbook contains a photograph sent to her of one such cross, which may be the one visited by Christina.

10. In fact, the cathedral would be rebuilt, as would the rest of the devastated town of Arras, with buildings of historical interest reconstructed exactly as they had been before the bombing.

11. Tunnels had been quarried out beneath the city of Arras for many centuries to provide stone for building. During the war these tunnels were extended to create an astonishing underground city where thousands of soldiers were based.

12

Closing down

Spring was coming – the daffodils in the woods all around told us that. The green of the sea too, was touched with silver where the spring sun kissed it; no longer were there white lines of foam between us and England. 'In the Spring,' the poet tells us, 'the young man's fancy lightly turns to thoughts of love,'[1] and no doubt with this admonition in view, the War Office belatedly bethought itself of us. It announced that by Easter, which this year fell towards the end of April, it would itself take over all Army Education in France. The decision was no surprise to us – it followed from education being established in the Army zones and in the Army of Occupation also. The document, however, conveying the decision, was a profound surprise to us. We had never realised the War Office thought so much of us: indeed, all evidence, as it drifted down pointed to the contrary. However, it was springtime and perhaps even the War Office felt it.

Anyhow, there I was one fine morning in the Chief's sanctum and there was he with his spectacles on his nose, reading a large official-looking document aloud to me. The War Office thanked us for conducting the Army Education with the great success we had. I opened my eyes! The Chief read stolidly on. The War Office was now going to undertake this important work itself. But it would never forget its debt to us: in fact, would the Chief give the thanks of the War Office to each member of his Staff and tell them that their 'courage and cheerfulness in the face of unexampled difficulties and hardships had been beyond all praise'. These latter words I learned by heart afterwards and tried to think that they had once been applied to me. They would be exceedingly useful to quote in future conversations with the Army brother. The SNO too, I made up my mind, should hear them word for word.

Meantime the Chief had taken off his spectacles and laid the document down. 'Pretty strong, isn't it?' he remarked.

'Strong!' I cried. 'They couldn't have said more if we'd worked in the trenches.' I was silent with awe. Then a misgiving came over me. 'Who has signed it?' I enquired. 'It may be only a hoax.'

He read out the name – unknown to me – of some general at the War Office. 'I don't suppose he has even seen anything of us,' I said doubtfully.

'I'm quite sure he hasn't,' the Chief agreed warmly, to my surprise. Then his eyes twinkled. 'But it's very nice for the papers, you know. Must make a great thing of Education if the War Office is going to tackle it itself.'

I sighed. 'I shall tell all the officers who come here that the War Office thinks our courage in tackling them is beyond all praise,' I declared, as I left the room.

The end had really come. The men were going home: so were many of the Hut Ladies: one or two Huts were already closed down: notices were up that the Garrison Church was to be given up at the end of the month. Not only so, but our own Chief on the Lines of Communication was going home in ten days' time.

For myself, a letter had come for me from my College in Oxford, asking how soon I could be back. Captain L. and I were making toast by the dining-room fire – a ceremony never fully understood by Marie Henriette who, like all Frenchwomen, saw nothing in toast – when I broke the news. 'They've offered me the Senior Tutor's rooms,' I told him, 'if I'll go back at once.'

Captain L. burst out laughing. 'Senior Tutor, indeed,' he cried. Marie Henriette, setting the table, looked benevolent but uncomprehending. '*Mademoiselle – moi, fiancés*,' ['*Mademoiselle* – I'm engaged'] said Captain L. with a wave of his toasting fork.

Other officers, hearing the laughter, drifted in. One of them caught me, toasting fork and all, and waltzed me round the table. 'Senior Tutor, indeed,' they cried. 'You're in France now.' For they one and all looked on my future life as worse than a convent, in that it held the added gloom of learning.

I straightened my hair. 'Oxford will indeed be very different from this,' I said, looking round the eager circle, 'but I'm going there all the same and maybe I shall like it.'

'We'll come and see you,' volunteered one, as if he expected me to ban his visit.

'Oh yes, I hope you'll all come,' I entreated. 'It will be so awfully dull at first.' But I did not realise then that Oxford would be bigger than us all, and that they could not come to me nor I to them in the different atmosphere across the Channel.

It was a wild March morning when the Secretary and I saw the Chief off. He was to motor to Havre.: only our librarian went oncataloguing the few books we had left Nearly all had been packed up in huge crates downstairs and were waiting, their labels in block letters stamped on their lids, to be sent to Cologne. But a soldier, a librarian in civil life, catalogued afresh those that were left, though anyone with a glance at the shelves could read the titles of the dozen books or so we still had. The Chief was muffled to the throat for his long journey: someone carried his souvenirs, someone threw in his luggage – a hurried shake of the hand and the Secretary and I stood alone on the doorstep; the Area Education in our own hands.

'What shall we do?' she said disconsolately, as we returned to her room. It was piled up with cigarette boxes and flowers, the gifts of the departing officers to us both.

A sudden thought struck me. 'I know,' I cried. 'We'll have a children's party to end up with, like the Demob people.'

'But we don't know any children,' she protested.

'There are lots here,' I retorted airily. 'Some were playing at that concert. I'll go and ask them this very afternoon.'

It was rather an odd errand, if I had thought of it, calling at people's houses and asking them to let their children have tea with us. I don't suppose any English parent, except of the poorer classes, would have listened to me for a moment. But the French were well used by this time to the English love of children – our School was well known in Dieppe – and I met with no refusal at all. Unknown though I was to all of them, I was received with great politeness and the children were promised for the day I asked. Such officers as were left were delighted at the prospect – they could not all come to tea, I pointed out, as our table was not big enough, but they might all come to play games afterwards. It was the one thing needed to cheer us up in the days we were passing through.

The children came and were not in the least shy: French children don't seem to be. They were indeed shocked at our extravagance in giving them butter and jam together and still more amazed at what they thought the liberality of the fare provided. But the games were the really interesting part: the officers spoke little French and the children no English, but when the game had been explained in both languages, the officers shouted in the children's French and the children in an odd word or so of English. When the party ended, the children begged to be invited back again, as with great reluctance they departed.

Only one happening of interest took place while we had charge of the School – the War Office requested us to carry on for another month – really, as we thought, because they were not at all ready to take over themselves, but on the pretext that we did it so well and that it was not worthwhile beginning with fresh instructors. But we politely declined.

And now in the prevailing atmosphere of farewells, I felt that the sooner I got home, the better. It would be hateful to remain until not a friend was left. So far I had still not got to Paris, but when I applied to the APM for permission to go home, I boldly added 'via Paris'. There was great excitement to know what would be done with this clause. Permission did not come till teatime the day before I was leaving, but on the permit there were written the magic words, 'via Paris'. In great delight I telegraphed my sister that I would be there for a few hours next day. It meant getting up at six a.m. to catch the Paris train and it meant risking the visé at Havre, as probably the British Consul would not be on duty when the evening train reached the port, and so I might be held up after all. But the alternative was most of the day alone in Havre, as the boat did not sail till night. And I was all for Paris.

I turned down the *Plage* for the last time about eight o'clock at night to say goodbye at the Headquarters for France. On the way I passed the Hôtel Métropole, where a few days before the City of Dieppe had entertained the English Base to a farewell reception and where the French had looked on openmouthed as we danced an eightsome to the pipes of the Glasgow Highlanders. At the Headquarters, which I had found such a Tower of Babel but six short months ago, I passed from room to room saying 'Goodbye' to one new friend after another. In one room a tall, rather handsome man in a trench coat stood talking, cigar in mouth, to a man I knew. He stared at me rather hard as I said, 'Goodbye', and then interrupted with, 'Going home tomorrow, are you? But my dear child you'll never do all that – Paris and the boat, you know.'[2]

'Oh, I can try anyway,' I said hopefully.

'Look here,' he said, taking the cigar out of his mouth. 'I'll make a bargain with you. Give up Paris and I'll motor you through to Havre tomorrow. I'm going home myself.' I hesitated. 'I've got a topping car,' he said lazily. 'Haven't I Smith? I've just come straight from Cologne.'

'I should love to,' I said slowly, 'but I do want to see Paris.'

'If you go there,' he went on, 'you'll have to stay in Havre, you know. There's no manner of chance you'll get the British visé that night.'

'Sure?' I asked.

'Dead sure,' he answered. 'Better come with me.'

'Thank you I will,' I plunged firmly.

'I'll be round for you at 11 a.m. tomorrow. Sleep well.'

He stared at me still till I left the room. The man I knew came with me. 'You'll be all right,' he reassured me with a laugh. 'He's a little sudden but that's all. But he'll take you to London all right and put you in the train for Scotland too.'

Truth to tell, I had had enough of facing French railway authorities, who either told me I was 'militaire' and so must travel by night, or said I wasn't militaire at all and refused to give me a ticket, and the thought that I would be taken care of appealed very greatly. I could see Paris another time. A glorious motor ride to Havre in plenty of time for the boat was not to be despised. So I slept the sleep of the lazy and wired to Paris that I was not coming.[3]

It was nearly noon before the car eventually turned up next day, with not only my new friend and his chauffeur on board, but two ladies as well, both, I suppose, collected as I had been. One was middle-aged and quite friendly to me. She had been a Leading Lady at the Huts all winter and with the 'airs of a duchess' had, I believe, a kind heart beneath them. She had remarkably little luggage, as she pointed out with pride, for so long a sojourn in France. She also was returning to England and I was rather relieved than otherwise to see her. But the second lady was a different type. A widow of uncertain age and rather youthful appearance, she was possessed of very lovely violet eyes, a mass of dark hair and a pale face. She had been out for four winters, and whatever may have been the case in the other three, her appearance now had the effect of emptying each hut she was sent to. If the soldiers were hungry enough or bold enough to remain, she wrangled with them as fiercely from behind the counter as ever I have heard fishwives do in my own country. Also she would not stand behind the counter, as we all did, but insisted on a cushioned armchair. The bête noir of the men, the siren of some of the officers, she was not over popular with the Hut Ladies. I had never actually met her before and surveyed her with apprehension. She, on the other hand, looked on the little crowd of uniforms who had come to see me off, with obvious disfavour.

My spirits rose as I settled in the car at the thought of what a strangely mixed party we were. My host looked already as if he now regretted asking me, when the violet-eyed widow, with the sigh of a martyr, made room for me beside her. We whirled out of Dieppe at a great pace, past the camps and huts I had grown to know so well, and I had already forgotten my company when there was a resounding groan and the car slowly came to a standstill. Our host descended. 'What is the matter?' he enquired of his chauffeur somewhat nettled. 'This car has never broken down before.'

I began to wish I had gone to Paris after all. Small French boys collected from nowhere and stood around with interest. Our host invited Violet Eyes to come and sit on the nearby bridge with him. The Leading Lady and I were left alone. After an interval he returned. There was an inn close by – would we all go there with him? The drive was obviously more than ever to his distaste. We were only five or six miles from Dieppe, but wild horses would not have taken him back there. To begin with, he was piqued at the car breaking down; and secondly he was angry with himself at being caught with three women all together. One at a time was his motto, and let the time be short, not three in a bunch as now, with no prospect of getting rid of any of them either. He was plainly cursing his own flirtatious disposition last night.

In the meantime, we adjourned to the inn for a sober repast of coffee and omelettes. At the end, Violet Eyes and our host went out, and now that the boat at Havre receded further and further into the distance, I resigned myself to extracting as much amusement as I could from the present. It was a fine day and the Leading Lady and I strolled out. The chauffeur was still tinkering with the car, which looked as if it had been reduced to its elementary parts. The road was strewn with bits of its insides. Our host and his fair lady were deep in conversation on the bridge. For six hours we waited, until at last a car was seen approaching from the opposite direction. Our host stopped it at once and after some colloquy, it turned round and we were bidden to get in. It was an Australian YMCA car – a beautiful touring Daimler – returning from Havre, where it had discharged its passengers. 'You must go straight back to Havre and in double-quick time,' the Australian driver was commanded. Here the Leading Lady and I humbly begged that our luggage too be transferred as our host showed signs of abandoning all our personal possessions and urging on the driver at the butt of a revolver. Violet Eyes was only going to Havre for a joyride and had no luggage. Our request was curtly granted and we started off at last.

This time our host must needs sit by Violet Eyes, not by the driver. This arrangement put the Leading Lady in the front while I – being rather small – squeezed into the corner in the shelter of our host's large back, his face being turned towards the charmer. My heart now was set on Havre, as firmly as ever Queen Mary's had been on Calais, and all my hopes of courtesy from our host had vanished into a lazy sort of curiosity as to whether he would kiss her before or after we had got to Havre, and whether she would let him do it openly.

We flew along the long straight roads, past village and hamlet, skirted the coast, whirled and flew and whirled again and then really, at long last, the lights of Havre did begin to appear. It was almost too good to be true and I just sat up and shook myself awake when the car stopped in the centre of the town. We all got out; my luggage was dumped down on the pavement, the Leading Lady picked up her suitcase and our host came up to me. 'There, now,' he said, looking down at me, 'I've done what I promised. I've taken you to Havre. Good night. I'll see you on the boat.' And they all walked away – leaving me '*plantée là*' as the French say, with my luggage on the pavement.

I looked around for a cab. There was none in sight, nor any likelihood of getting one, judging by their scarcity all over the North of France. While I looked, I heard a voice address me. 'Say, aren't you with these folks or have they left you?' It was the Australian soldier driving the car.

'They've left me, I'm afraid,' I said with a rueful smile. 'I suppose you couldn't take me to the boat, could you?' I asked him tentatively.

Before I had the question well out, he was down on the pavement picking up my luggage and stowing it in the car. 'Now,' he said, holding the door open for me, 'I guess we'll just go on anywhere.'

'Trust the Army,' I said to myself. 'They'll never let you down.'

We drove slowly along brightly lit streets until we struck an English military policeman, who directed us to the docks, and in a few minutes we were there, and at the quay before us lay the *Antonia* ready to take us home.

I made for the AMLO – could I leave my luggage? He surveyed my dusty and dishevelled figure with a kindly pity, then came out to inspect the luggage. It was a small black trunk, now completely veiled in dust and with its bottom nearly knocked out through much jolting in the car. The silent Australian lifted it off and the Sergeant turned to me. 'You'll never get this to England, Miss', he told me. 'It'll be broke in bits long before then.' I suppose I looked about to cry at the news, for he added, 'Never mind, missie. I'll look after it. I'll sew it up in sacking for you and it'll go over OHMS. It'll be all right that way.'

'Will you really?' I breathed.

'Sure thing,' he answered. 'You look out for me before the boat goes.'

It appeared the boat would not leave much before midnight. Boats are, in this way, so like their sex: you never know what they are going to do. '*Varium et mutabile*' [Fickle and changeable] came into my head at that moment – now with a train, though the heavens fell, it would leave at or near the scheduled moment. With heartfelt thanks, I said goodbye to the Australian and moved across to the Shipping Office in the hope of getting a cabin. By a piece of luck, I got one of the best deck cabins and much relieved, made for the local Education centre, where I knew the Chief – an English Professor who had often invited me to visit him and whose admiration of the Argyll and Sutherlands had been so profound.[4] With open arms he welcomed me, gave me dinner, introduced me to his Secretary who pleaded with me to stay all night. I confessed I might have to, as my passport was not *viséd*.

'Not *viséd*,' they cried. Oh, but they knew the APM. The Secretary herself would come down with me to the boat and see him. So in the education car down I spun to the boat again, and got on board first of all the passengers. There was no sign of the YMCA host or of Violet Eyes. Presently they drew up and to their great surprise beheld me, passport *viséd*, luggage on board care of the Army, deck cabin engaged, car that had brought me waiting at the quay. I confess I was pleased. Our host looked blank. 'Oh, so you managed,' he said.

'Yes,' I replied demurely, 'I managed.'

In the blue darkness the lights gleamed – the lights of peace. The low sound of the sea sucking the *Antonia*'s keel came up to me. French voices mingled with English: when the dawn came, I reflected, it would rise for me in England. France and all it stood for would be far behind. There would be no more RTOs to help me over the rough places, no more soldiers to be proud of me and to make me proud of them. I should meet again rude women and indifferent men, and there would not be the Army by my side to retrieve me from the shock. After that night I should never again be 'Care of the British Army'. Though I said these things over and over again to myself, I did not realise them. How could I, with the Sergeant coming up to see if I had a nice deckchair and to tell me that my luggage was sealed and sewn and would carry to the end of the world! And how could I indeed, with Violet Eyes in the dusk lifting her white face to our host a few yards away and the sound of broken voices drifting across to me. For that too was France. In England tomorrow it would not happen. For England stood for other things. Thackeray knew France too, and he sang:

> The reddest lips that ever have kissed
> The brightest eyes that ever have shone
> May pray and whisper and we not list
> Or look away and never be missed
> Ere yet ever a month is gone.[5]

For I knew that England would bring that too – it was a clean slate for the Army and for me, when we came home again. Memory is short – it cuts both ways – and English traditions would hold when we got over the water.

But, lying back in my deckchair, I knew that Life would never again hold anything as good for me, as it had held these six months in France. I had met all kinds of people that in England I should never have known; I had learnt what seemed to me most amazing things – to flirt, to be made love to, to nurse, to cook, to be friends with quite uneducated people without feeling in the least superior to them, to sleep in empty houses without feeling frightened, to know that a man will 'kiss the lips that are near' whether he be married or not, and to accept the fact. I had learnt too that good people were infinitely more numerous than I had supposed, that they didn't look it, and that it was nothing short of a miracle how good they were.

All these may seem but trifling things to have learned; but they are not so really. In the ordinary orbit of experience, one is rarely so detached from one's circumstances as to be able to meet people while one remains a complete non-entity oneself. The label is rarely absent from the observer and is sometimes all that those who are with him, react to. But in France no one knew whether I was rich or poor, good or bad, educated, religious or the reverse. I was simply an English girl and people approached me under each of those characters. I was offered money, very tactfully I will admit – I was assumed to possess a maid and dine at the Carlton. I was invited – perfectly frankly – to come to Paris by a married officer, as if it was a quite ordinary proposition, and to my life-long surprise I nearly went; I was more decorously invited to be the wife of others; I was treated with great affability and some condescension by people who in England are the strictly segregated tradespeople; I had dined with an Oxford don and found him dull, with an ungrammatical Sergeant and found him thrilling; I had played hymns at Evangelistic meetings that would have sent cold shudders down academic backs; I had looked with the rapture expected of me at boxing matches and melodramatic 'pictures'; I had listened to high regimental officers making fools of themselves over classics and humble private soldiers toiling at the same with love; and ever through the phantasmagoria, here, there and everywhere, came the people I had loved. Every day and every place, there seemed to be fresh ones and always dearer because of the background of tragedy from which the men came and the background of evanescence that showed up the women.

Tomorrow, we would all be where? One a mannequin in London, Circe to a girls' school in Calcutta (Circe of all people!), the Lady of the Lovely Hair would return to a husband and a grass hut in Central Africa, one would go to China as a Secretary and me to a High Table in Oxford, to chaperone the young and foolish. The cards were well shuffled and the world is wide; but the face that stood out clearest, as the *Antonia* weighed anchor and headed back to England, was the face of the officer who had wanted me to go to Paris and whom I had sent back to his wife:

> She said, 'Now kiss me and be going
> My sweetest dear
> Kiss me this once and then be going
> For now the morning draweth near.'

> With that the shepherd waked from sleeping
> And spying where the day was peeping
> He said 'Now take my soul in keeping
> Since I must go, since day is near.'[6]

At breakfast time we steamed into Southampton and at lunch I faced the Principal over the High Table and expressed my pleasure that the Scholarship candidates – girls of 17 and 18 from English High Schools – *Dio Mio!* – would be ready to be interviewed that afternoon. It is our life in Oxford.

Notes

1. 'Locksley Hall' by Alfred Lord Tennyson.
2. This man, whom she later describes as 'the host', is not a member of the army but is with the YMCA.
3. Christina may have wired to Julia and Mildred in Paris that she was not coming, but they never received the message. Mildred wrote to her mother on 12 April: 'We expected Tiny on Tuesday and luckily I was unable to get away and go to meet her at Gare St Lazare as she did not turn up at all. Jul and I were both to have had the afternoon off that day, but neither of us could get away before 1 p.m. It is a pity she wasn't able to come here as she would have loved seeing the [Hotel] Majestic and as it happened there was a singularly distinguished party at lunch that day.'
4. This 'Chief' was the area sub-director for Le Havre, Professor Medley.
5. 'The Age of Wisdom' by William Makepeace Thackeray.
6. 'The Wakening', John Attye's *First Book of Airs*, 1622.

13

L'Envoi

Weeks afterwards the poem that follows arrived for me:

La belle Marguerite at St Hilda's

You tell me of the scented hours
When memories of a gayer land
Come dancing o'er the trees and towers
That make your Oxford green and grand.

I do not blame; nay, I should laugh
If ever I could chance to meet
On a St Hilda's garden path
A Don, and with her, Marguerite.

And I should watch you as you walk
Along the sheltered river-side
You pouring out high-table talk
And shewing Magdalen's storied pride.

And she responds 'How wise' 'How fair!'
Then she will give a little sigh,
As if she wanted fresher air
And something that is not so 'high'.

Then, with a swift-shot, sidelong glance
– A glance that is a shy caress –
She whispers but the one word 'France'
And all your heart cried out with 'Yes!'

The scene dissolves as in a dream;
A straight road, poplar-fringed and white,
Where was the brown meandering stream,
And you are racing through the night!

Your pulses quicken as you ride;
What can you answer but 'you may',
As life holds out its arms so wide
To carry you away – away?

Marguerite is smiling through it all
– A smile that almost is a kiss!
Then suddenly – the curtains fall
And you are back again to *this*.

To Oxford and its perfect peace,
To Hilda's and her guarded ways,
To ancient love of Rome and Greece,
To donnish and to decorous ways.

'Tis evening, and, to evensong,
The Cowley bell calls through the air;
It is not that you have done wrong,
But you are hardly fit for prayer.

Is it not really more than this?
Was even *that* the true, the whole?
You'll say 'twas something not to miss
Yet – let me put it to your soul –

Might not *it* rather miss the more
Where all is reckoned up and told?
Lady – I feel I only bore,
Moreover, I am growing old.

(PS If you – by any chance,
Some other day, again should meet,
That lady friend of yours from France,
Please give my love to Marguerite.)[1]

Notes

1. This poem sums up perfectly the tension Christina felt between the stately
   reserve of Oxford life and the whirlwind freedom of her six months in
   France – so perfectly that it leads to the suspicion that she may have written
   it herself. Her brother, in his notes on the manuscript, is quite sure that this
   is not the case. Christina apparently kept the original with her for forty-five
   years until her death, and Barrogill goes on to say: 'The poem quoted in
   L'Envoi is not in the author's handwriting and obviously was sent her by one
   of the friends she had made in France. I do not know who the writer was
   but I thank him for it.'

Afterword

Lying back in my deck chair, I knew that Life would never again hold anything as good for me, as it had held these six months in France.

Christina took up her position at St Hilda's College, Oxford, and remained there for the rest of her university life. She expected a high standard of her students, who included not only those who had chosen to do Honours in Latin or Greek but also many who reluctantly studied Latin as a requirement of an Arts degree. Her teaching was thorough, but also tended towards the dramatic and descriptive.

She never married – despite the existence among undergraduates of a 'Society for Marrying Miss Keith'. As she grew older she became more idiosyncratic, and one college obituary described her as 'someone about whom legends rose'. Although comfortable in the academic environment, there is a sense that her spirit still longed for something more. Maybe it had something to do with the Caithness winds and wide horizons which had shaped her early days. She looked beyond the confines of the university, and became involved in teaching inmates in Oxford's prison in a move which surely held echoes of her Dieppe experiences. She also continued to travel. In 1925 she embarked alone on a world cruise, and wrote a series of letters to her mother, describing the ports of call, her fellow passengers and their experiences with her customary vivid colour.

In 1942 Christina left both Oxford and the Classics behind. She returned to Caithness, and devoted herself to the subjects which had perhaps been her first love all along – Scottish history and Scottish literature. Living alone in Thurso and relying on the Pentland Hotel for her meals, she wrote newspaper articles and published *The Russet Coat*, a study of Robert Burns. The reviewers did not quite know what to make of Christina's perceptive insights wrapped up in her unconventional style. Her history of Barrogill Castle, published when that castle came to prominence as the Castle of Mey, the Queen Mother's new home, was deeply personal, drawing on her family knowledge. A biography of Walter Scott, *The Author of Waverley*, was completed just before her death in 1963, and was seen through publication by her brother Barrogill.

Christina's story of her six months in France, at a time when soldier and civilian alike were beginning to shake free from the horror of war, is the story not just of a fascinating episode in history, but also of the triumph of women's education and the move towards a society less bound by convention.

For Christina, it was simply the story of a quite remarkable time in her life.

Appendix:
David Barrogill Keith

And tomorrow, oh! tomorrow, I thought, as I laid my tired body with rapture on my bed, tomorrow I shall see where my brothers have been and all the things they've never told me of these weary years.

As Christina travelled across the silent, charred landscape of northern France, she passed where her brother Barrogill had lived and fought while the guns still roared and the horrors of trench warfare were all around.

Barrogill may have told her little, but his mother Katie kept many of his letters from the front.

An accomplished artist with a keen sense of humour, Barrogill passed long weary hours in the army by drawing countless caricatures of his comrades. These little books evoke a real sense of the camaraderie which helped to carry the men through their terrible experiences. Comedy is laced with tragedy, as below many of the cartoons he has added the eventual fate of his friends – *killed at Dardanelles … killed at Salonika … wounded at Dardanelles …*

A sample of these pictures is reproduced here along with Barrogill's letters.

2.10.15
Royal Pavilion Hotel, Folkestone
My dear Mother,
I have arrived here on my way to France. We got word late on Thursday evening
that we were ordered off. We had no previous warning of any kind. A memo had
indeed come asking for all the names of officers fit to command active service
platoons but our reply had not reached Headquarters when we were ordered
off. There are 21 of us in all. We expect to be sent to different regiments.

I saw Mildred in Edinburgh on Friday morning and Jul in London this morning. I had of course no time to go north.

I am just writing this prior to catching the boat across so have not time to
say much.

There are several rumours afloat. One is that we are to make a new landing
at Ostend. Another that no more drafts are to be sent across later this year as K
wants all his men across now. What the reason of this sudden bustle is I don't
know. I only know that the Tain crowd are here too and from everywhere there
are crowds of officers so it may be that the hour has struck when K and Joffre
have determined to make the beginning of the end.

Personally I fear not. It seems to me that things are pretty black. What is a gain
of 200 or even 600 yards or even one mile or two miles. If we have only made
'em give ground we have gained nothing in the wide world. The time will be
when one or other drives a wedge through the other's line. Then the war will
be decided.

Meantime I must close. You might make up my comforter and balaclava
helmet – two pairs socks one pair or two pairs woollen gloves and send them
when I know my address.

You might also get Donnie to send me every week 50 Gold Flake cigarettes –
as soon as I am settled.

Meantime hoping everyone is well and don't worry too much as worry won't
help.

With love to all from DB Keith

5.10.15

12th Scottish Rifles, attached 10th Cameronians, BEF

My dear Mother,

There is nothing much to tell this time. Only yesterday I saw the fattest man in all the world. Honestly you could put five or seven men together in the space he occupied. He was simply enormous.

We hear the guns all day here but pretty far away in the distance. Other than that and the fact that this French town is full of khaki, one would not know of the existence of the war.

Things apparently are black in the Balkans. Bulgaria is in and probably now the other states will wait to see how the cat is going to jump. Greece may or may not come in. I think she probably will. Romania I think will not.

So public opinion seems to be rather against our success. The war anyway is hardly started. I do not believe the economic factor will defeat Germany. Germany is far too systematic to fail to take all due precaution against that. Some day a year or so hence *we* may awake to the fact that danger threatens us from that source. Of course so long as we retain control of the sea – with our colonies not going bankrupt through excessive pay to their soldier and bonuses and pensions and dependants – we ought to get our necessaries all right. But things are not looking too well and even on sea I fear the Germans. They have something up their sleeve. The war indeed – the more I see of it makes me more certain – will be a long one and the people to carry it to a close will be other men and other politicians.

It may be a day or two before I write again as there is nothing to report. You might arrange to send me some grouse and some other eatables now and then. Later when we have a company mess I might get some stuff sent out every day.

Love to all and hoping all is well.

From DB Keith

You'll see George on Tuesday I expect. DBK

11.10.15

My dear Mother,

I got your welcome letter this morning. I have tried to write as often as I can but we are pretty busy with one thing or another to get settled up and unfortunately my last letter to you did not get sent off as soon as it might have.

We are in a quiet place here but every day and night you hear the big guns booming just a continuous rumbling, something like bubbles on boiling toffee some big and some small – that's rather an absurd metaphor but it expresses what I mean – a sort of sultry series of eruptions. And at night flashes blink for a second across the sky. Aeroplanes often come buzzing around. A series of trains with unearthly shrieks of agony in lieu of whistles and proceeding at a mild walking pace tugging interminable trucks puff along across the level crossing just as one wants to cross. Occasionally motor buses – Red X or otherwise, a few French horsemen or a cyclist or two flit past. Otherwise things are as usual.

There are rumours pretty nearly always that we are being moved the next day, sometimes to the trenches, and we look with a kind of questioning wonder at the flashes across the sky, sometimes further back and we think of theatres and pleasant billets, but so far neither has eventuated, and we are still pegging away here and it's not so bad. We had a church service today to the sound of guns. It's all new and the experience of this war will, if I come through all right, make a tremendous difference in me. It may drive me insane or it may be the making of me.

We are starting our own company mess here and I want you to send out or rather get Munro or one of the keepers to send out *every day* a box of grouse, venison, partridge, duck, etc, anything – enough for four persons, say one [?] grouse today and partridges or duck or venison – just a small bit for four or six each day – can you manage that. Otherwise we are likely to live on bully beef. Parcels take three or four days I believe so the stuff sent should be newly killed if possible. The other fellows are getting parcels everyday but it's shortbread cakes honey etc.

16.10.15

My dear Mother,

For the last few days we have been pretty busy and I had no opportunity to write a letter. I sent a dozen pcs to the family generally of scenes of the war etc. They will be interesting to keep. I have now lost immediate touch with George but he is still somewhere in the neighbourhood.

Life here tho' not devoid of excitement is not particularly interesting or daring. Apart from continuous gun firing and aeroplanes hovering overhead everything is much as usual. I have not yet seen a shell burst on the ground tho' I have seen some aeroplanes and observation balloons shelled.

The grouse and butter arrived all right and are now duly eaten, but so far there is no word of cigarettes. I have also got, as I think I told you before, my scarf and some woollen things direct from home. Nothing has been forwarded from Stobs [a training camp in the Scottish borders].

I will return the photos you sent next letter. Meantime they are packed in my kit. I had of course already seen them at Stobs.

Hope everyone is keeping quite well at home. So you are still having runs with Strachan. I really think he's too much swollen head. He will, I expect, learn it pretty soon from the people round about. The *Courier* seems to show that the people are about fed up with those self-conscious stay at home heroes who on active service require all the comforts of first-class hotels, if possible at the expense of the state.

You might let me know if the postcards arrive all right.

What's doing at home – everything pretty dead & alive?

If you are sending any stuff out here to Tommies don't send sweaters, cardigans, shirts, socks, etc. Any amount of these, as many as the people care to ask for are supplied free to the troops here. I know this for a fact. If they don't get them it's because their Quartermaster is rotten. But send out old magazines, matches and cigarettes. They get 50 cigs a week fewer than 500 each but these are all of one class and Tommy gets fed up without his Woodbine and his Gold Flake for variety. Send them of course cigarettes out of bond if possible. Also send 'em eatables but the people knitting are absolutely unnecessary. On active service if the officers are worth their salt and the QM a good man Tommy wants for nothing in the way of necessaries either of food or dress. But he wants luxuries, his own luxuries, little things such as handkerchiefs and soap. He gets plenty towels, a sponge, and odds and ends – reels, even small knives and forks for Tommy loses these and is looked on with a wrathful eye when he seeks that which was lost from comrades and Quartermaster.

No more just now, am just off to bed for this is really Thursday night tho' it won't go till tomorrow wherefore the date.

Hoping all are well, with love from DB Keith

Tuesday?

At last I am at the end of my wanderings at least for the time being. I am now within sound of the guns but quite far away from them and in absolutely no danger and likely to be in none for a month at best.

I met George today and was at his billets and saw him at teatime again. I have also been toddling about with Georgeson and have met Taylor who is in George's company and also seen a fellow Ross I used to know in Edinburgh. Altogether it has been most interesting. The division we are in is resting after Loos.

I heard that AS Pringle – who was north with Keith Fraser – has been badly hit. He was magnificently game. With a battleaxe and a revolver old Toosie got over the trenches. He was hit four or five times and still fighting when last seen. He was in command of the OTC when I joined. George was not in it. All seconds in command of whom George is one, were left behind before the attack. Later I believe George went up. My impression of him is that he makes an exceedingly good officer and is quite worthy of his job.

I don't think there is much to say now. We are just settling down here and quite behind the firing line with the certainty of a long rest.

Hope all are well. Love to all, from DB Keith

18.10.15

My dear Mother,

I got letters today from Tiny, Willie and yourself and yesterday from Mildred and Louise for which much thanks.

I thought I had acknowledged the grouse and butter. I got them and forthwith they were eaten.

Tomorrow George comes to dinner with us and if the partridges arrive as expected we will do well.

Other than the grouse and butter no eatables have as yet arrived and we have open-mouthed waited to find a parcel but none arrived. Never mind stuff. I'll have to send some of the stuff I have here back but eatables need not be carried save on the person.

I'm in billets all right and quite comfortable – see little of war in its actuality.

I'll write again tomorrow or later tonight, meantime I must end as the light is out and dinner ready.

With love to all and hoping all are well, from, DB Keith

23.10.15

Tho' it is only 9 p.m. I am fearfully tired and ready for bed. I got your budget of letters and one from Mil all right also one from Julia I think.

The partridges have not yet come to hand. I got the grouse yesterday, also truffles & honey pretty squashed 1 fowl and brace partridges. We ate 1 brace grouse yesterday, gave the other brace to the CO and the partridge and the fowl were eaten tonight.

The days here soon pass. The big guns are not far off and the flash lights up the sky very brightly and the […] of the shells thro' the air all help to make one realise the war. But for active service it is as yet pretty much a picnic.

I will write to Cox as father suggests. Also it might be better to give him a power of attorney over any stick, etc in my name.

I really am too tired to write more and must get off to bed.

I shall be sending home some things as I have too much out here. I fear George won't get home this time after all. Georgeson may have told that he met me.

With love to all and hoping all are well, from DB Keith

PS Can you let me have Saroléa's *Address to the French Class*? We don't have much to read here.

2.11.15

My dear Mother,

I have regularly got your letters and very frequently your parcels for which I have to thank you very much. The last parcel I received from you contained a brace of grouse and a piece ham which was much enjoyed. However, don't send any more ham as we get loads of it and jolly good stuff too. I also got a third parcel from Tiny which was also excellent. I am indeed very well off in respect of parcels for which many thanks. The CO and I had many meals off the grouse and partridges arriving while we were in the trenches. We go in again in a day or two so a repetition and continuous feast will be most acceptable. You will remember also to keep a turkey and grouse for Xmas.

About stuff for the men honestly they want absolutely nothing. They get a brand new rigout every time they come out of the trenches. They get a ration issue of cigarettes. They get papers and presents. I can honestly think of absolutely nothing in the way of ordinary comforts that you could send them that would be of any use. Parcels of eatables are of course asked for when they write home but then you can't cater for that.

About my stove at home the only one that is any use out here is a PRIMUS paraffin stove. I had one once, a small pocket one. It seems to have got lost. If you find it you could send it otherwise don't bother. I really don't need one, only if there was that one knocking about unused we could use it. I don't think it is tho' and a metholated stove is useless and an ordinary paraffin one too heavy to take about.

I am sorry that Father has a cold and Ed the mumps. However I hope both are now better. You will see Foulis got wounded, a soft 'cushy' one we call it. It means a slight wound enough to let him get home and do no damage. He is as right as rain.

That last tour in the trenches was more or less uneventful. Except for dodging shells and one strafe of our own it was monotonous. One day an attack was reported and I had the messages calling up our artillery written out. It didn't come off. I have the messages and later when ancient history will send you the identical message which will be interesting to keep. I have also drawn rough sketches of my dugout. You might ask Poll next time she is in Princes Street to go to DOIG WILSON & WHEATLEY in I think Castle Street on the left-hand side going down and buy a small *6d* ricepaper sketchbook or perhaps 1s and a good drawing pencil, a soft one to make sketches here.

You could send out one or two 7*d* or 1*s* novels; they always help to clear the monotony of existence.

Well I must end up now as I have some more letters to write. Love to all, thanks for the parcels. Hope all are now quite well. With love from DB Keith

10.15

My dear Mother,

George is taking this letter across with him when he goes on leave tomorrow. I hope he has a good holiday as he has had a pretty rotten time on the whole here with all his chums knocked out.

Things are rather quiet here on the whole and tonight we leave billets to go into the trenches, but it is improbable that things will be busy where we go as we got a pretty severe knock so lately.

However as now I am in command of my company I will have a great deal to do and won't get many letters written even if facilities for posting them occur so don't worry if you don't hear from me for ten days or so. It will certainly do nobody good. Of course nowhere in the trenches is absolutely safe but still it's not very bad in the support and not in the firing line. But we will be awfully busy working there and with no sleep at night I may find my hands full.

I get on very well here on the whole. The adjutant was going on leave on Friday or Saturday and I was to be acting adjutant in his stead. Now in all probability leave is off.

Well I can't say much more as after all there is little to say. This time next week I will have either settled down to the trenches or be sick. Somehow I feel I will like the change into the trenches. After all my years at the Varsity were fighting ones and I was ever a fighter so one fight more. In all the things I have tackled, tho' I says it as shouldn't, I have fought with all my soul and I have tho' the honour is not mine, in all won through. And here now on the verge of this trench war I feel a strength and confidence that I hope and believe will carry me thro' so that at all events you will not I hope have cause to be ashamed of how I faced the foe.

This must be all as it is now about 11 and I have to go across to George with this and after that probably more work.

I have the honour of taking 'A' Coy into the trenches with only one other officer to help me and this tho' another officer arrived tonight but had he been posted to A would have taken over command. Fear not I'll win this all right.

Best wishes and love from DB Keith

4.11.15

My dear Mother,

You are no doubt wondering why I have not had time to write you, and what has been doing here. Well to start from the beginning George left for home and I turned towards the firing line the morning after his departure. Then I roosted for 12 days clad fully and never having clothes or boots off. Mostly it was wet, mostly it was cold, mostly it was slightly dangerous but it was grand.

Sleep of course was at a minimum; on two days I had none at all on other days 4 hours or so. Yet it was an excellent experience. You would I am afraid have looked rather askance at me had you seen me on my way back to billets here. The trenches were muddy, so muddy that even my knees were thick and at times it looked as if it would require some effort other than mine own to pull my huge feet out of the treacly toffee stuff.

However at length we saw daylight, toddled over the open ground and it rained. We were still toddling we splashed quite contentedly thro' two feet of water with light hearts but wet clothes and chilled stomachs. But when we got back we had some feed. I rather wished that I could have been photographed there tramping back in the darkness over what was once a road tho' now thro' ruts mostly a ditch.

But to return. The first things that gave me the real sense of a nation at war was on the march to the trenches. There was the youth of France, lads of 12 to 15 with coats off digging holes at the roadside to drain off the water. There they were digging trenches. It is a marvellous war.

Comparatively small children whom one accustoms oneself to think of as always laughing and playing football, wee kids with serious faces and muddy legs dig dig digging for the war had made even them helpers of their country.

Well we got to behind the firing line, to see what was once a town about the size of Thurso. Houses clean and new looking but only irregular chunks of wall left standing. In the gardens behind open gates and painted railings were pear and apple trees, with foliage but no fruit. The fruit no doubt unripe enough in its early youth, had been plucked by a hungry Tommy to the disgust of the R&AMC [*sic* – RAMC]. The church was still standing only half the tower was not. The door was open but I question if anyone had entered it for months. The windows were gone long ago and stones and masonry heaped the floor. Yet not so long ago some priest had it for his chapel. The Crucifix was visible thro' the open door. But there is neither priest nor populace there any longer. Instead Guns, Guns, Guns, and a RED X Ambulance and a British graveyard with its wooden crosses.

We got into the communication trench and passed on from dusk to darkness and we heard the rifle bullets singing and saw the flares and we knew we were in it at last. I slept in a small hole in the earth 6x4x4 ft. There we messed and ate the grouse and partridges you sent and always watched for the Boche.

I gathered lots of souvenirs. A German rifle with cartridges. An Austrian with fixed bayonet, an old battle bludgeon with its head studded with nails such as the sturdy yeomen of England went forth to wage war with to France in other days, and the noses of all kinds and conditions of shells.

These I left. To carry what one needs is bad enough, to carry these is impossible.

After a day or two we transferred nearer the firing line, now about 100yds from the Boche. Here we resided in a gorgeous dugout, once the pride of a German officer, a spring mattress, tables, chairs, wooden walls, everything excellent – and at the side a door to another compartment with a cupola in it of ½" steel with snipers' windows which could be opened and shut. The Boche does nothing by halves. Later I found another dugout where he had electric light. Really the conveniences of war sometimes are nice. But the awfulness of never taking clothes off. Always on the alert, never sleeping or sleeping but little makes one soon tired. After a day or two again I moved forward still further till I was only 20yds from the Genial Boche in this trench. Here, as you may imagine, I did not sleep, nor was there any hole in the wall into which I could creep, did I so desire. It rained all day and all night and I waited then for the dawn right thro' the night, watching the parapet of the Boche. Dawn at last, and with it I scour the trench opposite with my glasses and in the dim light observe a too venturesome German who I send away, I think, in an ambulance. He was not far away. He was still. He offered a good target. I am a passing shot. I took my time and he disappeared.

Daytime it was not bad at all, especially getting dry. Night again and again anxiety, and an attack. About midnight or 1 a.m. the Boche and his bombers crept up and we blazed like billy oh, and he did not reach our trench. After that quietness, but eternal watching. Then I went back to 100yds from the Boche and had a decent sleep and rest, what time he expended many shells which we received with fatalistic contempt.

Some days later we were relieved and toddled thro' mud and mud and mud, thro' narrow trenches, over-hanging wire, and watery roads to the musical accompaniment of shells, shells, shells.

Our turn in the trenches was exciting. With the Boche only 30yds away we often indulged not indeed in chucking stones or mud but in pushing some bombs over, a job at which I have now hard actual experience, tho' I fear not to the material damage of our enemy however much to his mental discomfort. One afternoon I went and threw a few at him and he threw more back so we shut up.

At another part of our line we have heaped sandbags. The Boche 15yds away along the same trench has done ditto. Both sides have loopholes and each looks with interest thro' these iron holes to see how the other is behaving. The Boche indeed asked us over to tea on more than one occasion, an invitation neither accepted nor reciprocated.

With it all, all the hardships and all the danger of which latter curiously enough one feels little except when one is lonely, it is a great and strenuous and topping life. Really it is great. Everything is against you, it is man and ingenuity against Nature and Climate with a dash of venomous Boche. I was out burying some people too and thought nothing of it. My first day in the trenches I was watching the enemy over the dead body of an Essex man lying on our parapet. Later when close to the Germans the trenches smelt horribly in places of dead Boche. Yet one does not mind, tho' after a bit one looks forward for the day when one gets back to dry land and billets. The rain is very bad.

We return to the trenches to relieve I think George and his brigade one day quite soon. Perhaps I may have time to write again. I have got lots of parcels from you which were excellently opportune. I got one from Tiny. It's awfully jolly getting these things and makes life somewhat better than eternal salt bully beef.

You will be pleased to hear I am now adjutant of this battalion. It means extra pay and possibly more comfort and less danger with enough to obtain my share of honour. I go of course to the firing line as usual but no patrols or visiting sentries, etc while things are humming. I only sit at the phone and talk, talk, talk. I believe the gazette will come out sometime this year if War Office take their usual efficient celerity. It means however a stop to my promotion, but it is better to take it and chance getting something out of it. At present till my gazette comes out, I am of course acting adjutant.

I heard about father going to see sir. I hope everyone is well and that Ed is going to be a soldier.

It may surprise you, but there are indications to my opinion the war will be over within about three months.

Hoping everyone is well, with love to all, from DB Keith

6.11.15

My dear Mother,

I wrote you a long letter two days ago and I hope you got it all right. It exhausted most of my news and I have little left to tell. I have not seen George since his return and will not for some time. We are as I said going back and forward to the trenches in spells and go in very shortly. About the middle of December we go out for a month's rest so we will I hope spend Xmas and New Year in comfort and most probably quite pleasantly. About New Year time I qualify for leave and may get home. But that's quite a distance ahead yet!

Our Battalion got today a *Médaille Militaire* for one of its sergeants and DCM for another. We also got a Military Cross for one of our Lieutenants. So altogether we have done not badly out of the attack.

At present we are back in billets and are having quite a good time on the whole. I got a large packet of cigarettes in the trenches from Martins. They were not nearly so good as the packet from Jul. Cigarettes out here are none too plentiful tho' there is any quantity about. They are smoked day and night.

In the attack our men having rushed through the 1st and 2nd lines of German trenches, lit cigarettes and strolled up and over Hill 70. They got tired and sat about smoking so utter was the German rout. Now when as in the trenches we are up day and night we smoke a lot. So they are very welcome and the very kind I like and they will last for several weeks.

I got several letters from Tiny and also a parcel which was very nice of her. This was the 2nd parcel and I also got toffee from Poll very much appreciated. It arrived in the trenches.

Another fellow Waddy has taken over seeing about getting my book published and I must write to him about it.

The university book of caricatures is with you I think. It contains some people now who have become casualties – which makes it all the more interesting.

Coming under fire is not extra terrifying. In fact it doesn't disturb one at all, only heavy shelling is a bit uncomfortable if it comes too near.

Well I'm ending now. Hope all are well. Animals to eat are most in demand of all the stuff you send. Can you get my old watch sent out at once – the one I used to carry. This new one is bust again and I'm at sea. See if you can get a whalebone cover – not a metal one for it but send it as soon as poss.

Hope all well, love to all from DB Keith

9.11.15

My dear Mother,

Your letter and the parcel arrived last night. The grouse, etc were excellent. Unfortunately as has happened the last time the dish conveying the potted head got rather collapsible en route and the potted head, being mixed with splinters of glass was dangerous and therefore had with regret to be thrown away.

The Tomatoes also arrive mostly always the worse for wear.

I got several letters yesterday and was glad to hear that everything, bar the mumps of Edward John's, was all right.

Well you won't hear again from me for some days as we go into trenches proper tomorrow, being at present in a remnant of a town among guns and shells. Yet I abide in a house with a whole room in which I sleep and we are fairly comfortable.

I hope father is quite well and found Sir Archibald also well. I am feeling all right and should be very comfortable comparatively in the trenches, i.e. compared with last time.

Hope all are having a good time and you'll send us a turkey for Xmas. It isn't so awfully far off.

With love to all from DB Keith

11.12.15

My dear Mother,

I sent some days ago my watch home for repair. I enclosed two aluminium rings. Tiny asked for one some time ago so you might give her one, the other you might give to Louise. Later I will no doubt get others. My servant went on leave a day or two ago and he was to try and smuggle thro' a German rifle, a French bayonet and a fuse of a huge Boche shell. He was to send these to you. If they arrive you might give the rifle to Edward John, the bayonet will make a nice poker for the drawing room and the fuse will do for Will. There is no chance of getting a Boche helmet at present so I can't do anything in that way. I hope the things get through all right. I may send later on an empty shell case which makes either an excellent gong which it is used for out here or a flower vase. However, meantime I see no prospect of it getting sent home. Leave too is a bit in the air as very few of us are allowed away at one time. I will not know definitely for a few days how things are to pan out in that respect.

Parcels have been arriving with great regularity for which I am awfully grateful. Now, however, we are out of the trenches for a long time so it isn't at all necessary to send more as we can get stuff cooked easily.

About clothes for the trenches, I don't want waders we get issued with them already. But I will get a coat myself in London one of these days. Thorntons I have always found too ready to palm off not extra convenient stuff as for instance the waterproof sheet which they presented me with and which I have never used and is more or less absolutely useless owing to its tremendous weight. The first rainproof I got there was nothing special either, and the waterproof I got later was a good waterproof but not a good trench coat. However now I have had experience and I know what to get myself.

A large parcel of woollens arrived yesterday for which please thank everyone. It came in very handy and is now practically distributed and everyone seems pleased. It came just as we got out of the trenches and therefore was more appreciated than had we been living lives of ease in the reserve billets.

I intended when I started to write a long letter about our doings but I feel very tired and don't think I will just now. Tomorrow I'll do it if possible. What is happening at home – everything as quiet as usual and the Office very busy? Is Lord Derby's scheme doing anything in Caithness or are they still living in hopes that it is a dream that the country is at war. Anyway the way in which the ladies have worked for us out here shows that they realise, if others do not, the unfortunate fact of this war.

Well I really will stop now; I hope however all are quite well and father and granny keeping fit; with love to all from DB Keith

14.12.15

My dear Mother,

We are now well back from the firing line and have a top-hole billet – nice white sheets, white-lace pillows, etc, everything absolutely dinky. I am pretty busy it is true with office work but other than that we have a jolly time.

Never mind now about sending out stuff, we can get everything nicely. Never mind even about a goose or turkey. Only if there is one to spare.

I hardly think I'll get home for New Year and it may be a good time before I can get back as things are behind.

I am only scribbling this in a hurry.

Hope everyone's well with love to all from DB Keith.

20.12.15

This will be my Xmas letter as I hope it will succeed in reaching you just on Xmas day. It is to wish you all a Merry Xmas and a happy New Year. All the family will be at home I expect save myself but don't worry about me, I'm getting on all right and Xmas out here isn't desperately bad, except of course that it differs so far little from any other day in the week and like the weekly Sunday will arrive alas! without carols – and I am afraid quite with a shock. I can hardly realise that it is now three months since I have come out here. Time passes so quickly and this is not really war at all. For those in the trenches it's magnificent target practice carried out no doubt in the main by over zealous gunners engaged in what is I believe technically known as an Artillery Duel but which being interpreted means that our brave boys way back pow pow the Germans in his trenches and the German also way back pow pows our boys ditto. So we are the piano on which this elegant and oft recurring duet is performed and we don't like it one little bit. If our artillery and the Boche arranged to strafe one another and dodged about and hid well it would be more interesting and a glorious gentlemanly sort of procedure but for both the big fellows to whack us on the head with big sticks while we cower in the trenches and by mutual understanding refrain from punching each other is neither heroic laudable or funny. Still it's known as an Artillery Duel in Flanders!

Well I've a good deal to tell you. No doubt in that last letter of mine you were surprised at the proximity of the Boche. But in our last tour of the trenches he became quite friendly, he waved his arms, he threw white papers, he got up, he sat on his parapet, he came out of the trench altogether and one bold man came over to the regiment we relieved. They not to be outdone in daring sent out a bold L/Corpl too. These met in NO MAN'S LAND between the trenches while all the world wondered. They exchanged cigarettes, and the Boche told us we would be very welcome and well done to at his restaurant behind his barbed wire. But – the moment each parted they ran like billy oh for their respective little hole in the mud for the last blighter might receive some presents he didn't quite desire. Thereafter we had quite a chummy sort of time with Fritz, we threw over pamphlets inviting him to come and be happy with us and otherwise showed him how willing we were to have a guest. But the old blighter didn't come tho' grimy and unshaven and as he told us he had been there for months and months.

But during the night he must have been relieved as in the morn sullen mud and cold barbed wire and the ping of a rifle bullet were all the weather forecast we could get.

Curiously one of our fellows picked up a Boche shell fired at us indited I think R STRONG & CO. It must be a swine of an American firm but these Americans are poor fools anyway and not worth quarrelling with.

Well today I saw Field Marshal Sir John FRENCH for the first time saying his farewell to his troops. We were all drawn up along the roadway and presented arms as the car with the white-moustached old man passed slowly along. And then it passed away – for ever with the man who for eighteen months has charge of the British Destiny in France.

Last night we had a concert. But soldiers' concerts out here are different indeed from those at home. At home there are civilians and lots of smiling people in a well-lit hall. Here in Flanders it's a whitewashed schoolhouse with a stone floor, and the light is penny dips and the audience is only the khaki coated Tommy with his pipe in his mouth. Often they sing with no accompaniment and the predominant note is a dull low dreary melancholy about 'Dead for bread' or something of that sort. Be the song dismal, be the singer a bass and be there no accompaniment and roll the song on without rhythm thro' interminable stories of the woes of existence, the clamour and applause is great. Not that Tommy is downhearted or dull, on the contrary, but he is a bit of a sentimentalist as one understands as he joins with right good will in 'Dear Homeland – goodbye' or 'When Irish Eyes are Smiling' or other suchlike sentimental ditties.

But the pipes out here sound grand. It's a great thing to be a Scotsman and it's tremendous to be in a Scottish regiment with its pipes in this land of France. When the pipes play and we go swinging along we feel so much better than the poor, blue-coated Frenchy and we strut mightily proud thro' the streets of France. And at concerts with the tobacco smoke and the songs and the atmosphere it awakens memories of the great broad moorlands and the swirl of the wind and the clean sky and how we hate the Sassenach intruder. It must be the remains of that primitive instinct that made the Highland raiders come from their mists and their hilltops with their plaids wound tightly round them, and holding a good claymore come down into the lowlands to garner what they could by force and steel.

It's a great life this and it makes one realise the reality of humanity and how all men are equal and there are no classes and no schisms but all together doing their bit for the benefit of the whole. And yet there are officers and there are leaders and with the most democratic army in the world there is respect for the Officers aye, and tell it not to the labour parasite, there is love also; real deep affection between those in authority and the men they lead.

Well I'm getting off the point and only talking. We have an RC padre in the Brigade and he's absolutely Tip Top. No finer fellow could be imagined. He's Irish of course and he tells a good story and he's always giving and he's got a delightful brogue. Well he went on leave when the Calais Conference was on and got a divisional car down to CALAIS. There owing to mismanagement he couldn't get across because there wasn't any boat at all you see. So the other brass hats there they swore a bit and expressed themselves on the great staff capability of our army and the padre I'm afraid did likewise and then the happy thought of luncheon. Behold a big restaurant. Into this they strode and on opening the dining room door who should they find but Kitchener and the conference at lunch. The brass hats thought they would go and find some other little pub but the padre stood his ground. We're going to pay for what we eat he said so here goes. But to avoid any unseemly squabble no doubt K sent out and told them to come in and they came and dined in the same room. K was at the head of the table, Joffre on his right, AJ Balfour on his left and all the others round about but Sir John French was not there – only Sir Douglas Haig was. Lunch ended, K sent word that he was sorry that the transport had failed and if they liked the destroyer accompanying them was at their service.

Oho said the padre. I'm a bit of a sailor and I'll go. But the others trembled. The waves were very strong and the ship was very wee. However they took courage and embarked. Eight of them Colonels and such like were stuffed in a tiny cabin and battened down 'cause it was too rough for them to get out above. They were told that the ship was to start. It whistled and then they got off at an awful rate with unfortunate results to the inhabitants of that black hole. One elderly Colonel smashed his eyeglass, another stood upon his false teeth and the padre found his head on another's stomach, and it got worse and worse as the boat tossed and twisted and they all got as sick as dogs and they all rolled about mixed up on the floor and when they reached the other side – fortunately for the dignity of the British Army it was dark – they had to have ropes tied round their middle and get hoisted ashore.

Well I think I have drivelled enough now and I must stop. I hope you all have a jolly time and I will write again when Xmas has been and tell you all what it is like. There is nothing about leave yet.

With love to all and best wishes for Xmas, hoping all are well, from DB Keith.

20.1.16

Hotel Folkestone, Boulogne-sur-Mer

My dear Mother,

Here I am no further yet. We had to stay overnight at Folkestone and again overnight here and today we go up. I was not sick crossing but it was pretty rough. I saw Julia in London and Uncle John as no doubt they told you. I met Strang at Folkestone and we have stayed together all along. You might tell father he can draw £20 out of Coy if he wants as I have a balance of about £30 just now. The journey has not been too tiring with the frequent breaks. Well I'm just stopping now hoping you are all quite well, with love from DB Keith.

24.1.16

10th Cameronians BEF

My dear Mother,

Back in billets here again and going into the trenches very soon. We're awfully busy getting through old work that has accumulated.

I saw Julia and Tiny as I told you and had quite a good time. We had a big concert with George Grossmith, Harry Ainsley, Arthur Prince, Henry Leoni, etc – Gaiety London people here yesterday. It was very good indeed. Save it was rather out of place that the first song was 'Peace Time'.

I travelled back with Strang and saw Georgeson yesterday and today. There's nothing however to report. Hoping all well, with love from DB Keith

11.2.16

My dear Mother,

I got the grouse and rabbit and several letters and a parcel and letters from Tiny for all of which many thanks. About venison the last that came was quite good but slightly mouldy – but we cut that bit off and the rest tasted very good.

We have been out of the trenches now for several days and go back soon. It seems likely that before the middle of March the Germans will make a strong push – perhaps it will be their last effort, one really cannot tell.

We are having quite a good time here on the whole and I don't think I would change where I am if I could. I will try and write oftener but we are very busy indeed. I haven't seen George since he came out again and won't probably see him as we don't relieve his battalion this time.

I hope everyone at home is well and father keeping fit. I myself am as well as ever I was and we are quite a jolly crowd out here.

Today it's turned out wet but on the whole we have pretty good dry cold weather.

I see that the men at home are being called up and at last we look as if things were going to begin at home.

I hope to write again after but have no more to say at present. With love to all from DB Keith.

13.3.16

My dear Mother,

I haven't written now for some days. We are having quite a quiet time and the weather is not at all bad. I have got letters from Tiny and home pretty often and also parcels. Someone was asking eagerly who got the ring in Louise's cake; well I did – but nothing else. The CO got the button and sixpence. The MO the thimble. There was quite some fun over it. Oatcakes and shortbread are arriving regularly. It will be just about spring at home and things will be looking nice. Rather the most interesting part of the year this I think at home.

Here we are very quiet and the Hun isn't over assertive. We go out of the trenches tomorrow and get the first decent billets for a month. I haven't had my clothes off for a month save once for a bath! So you can imagine how we are looking forward to getting out. Afterwards there is talk of getting back again for a rest – which may or may not come off – we hope it will.

The French seem to be holding up the Boche attack at Verdun and things altogether look brighter but until the Boche has another good push I don't think he will be beaten. When he has pushed again and failed he'll soon own up I think. It's a good sign in one way that the Hun fleet came out and I hope we catch it and give it a good doing. The Boche will probably be very seasick after his long rest.

Leave is off at present, how long it will so continue I can't say but events anyway will move rapidly with the spring and time will soon pass.

Hope everyone is well and having a good time. They will all be home soon. Willie will probably get some leave before he joins his ship. What does he think about it?

Well it won't be long now I think before we get real summer out here. The days are lengthening out wonderfully.

I'll write again soon. The Division have refused my promotion so that's knocked on the head. With love to all, from DB Keith

16.3.16

My dear Mother,

We are now back in billets with the prospect of only two or three days more in the trenches before coming out for a long rest. On the whole we have had a quiet time enough and the weather these last days has been absolutely perfect – out in this Garden there are yellow daffodils; the sky is almost cloudless so I think winter is about passed now.

If you are having the same weather at home it ought to be lovely. The primroses will soon be out now. Olrig should be beautiful. Are you going to stay there this summer? It would be excellent – only with this Compulsion business, work in the office will be overwhelming.

I got a parcel from Pol I think today and your letter also one from Tiny. What is Will going to do? Is he passed out of the Naval College now altogether? I haven't seen George now for quite some time but we took over from his brigade last time we went into the line.

Archie would be in command of his Bn while Winston was at home. I wonder how he got on and how he is liked. I rather think they are in a healthier part of the line than we have had. Still there ain't much to choose especially if the weather is rotten.

Well I haven't any more to say just now, only hope you are all well and having a decent time, with love from DB Keith.

28.3.16

My dear Mother,

Well we are out of the line now for a little while and back at rest billets with the prospect of when we are again in the line all things wintry will have ceased – which is pleasant to look forward to. The last few days were exceptionally quiet. I don't think we have ever had a quieter time. But this tour in the trenches was pretty hard. Mostly we had snow and trenches were tumbling in and things were bad so everyone is jolly pleased to get out.

And we start a new regime. We're in a different Corps with the old sector – Col Ussher has returned which means I suppose Col Smith will get another regiment, anyway he will leave us and that is rotten luck as we couldn't have · a better CO no matter when we went to look for him even if it was in the 9th Div. The new people are installing new ideas. We're to become a kind of Prussian Guard – be nice and clean and look pretty. I suppose it's good for discipline but though it may work in summer it couldn't have worked in winter. And I don't know that we were very much worse off without all this polishing of buttons. Anyway there it is.

Leave is in an indefinite state, some days it's on and the next it's off. So I may or may not get home about the middle of April.

I haven't seen George lately and don't know how he is getting on tho' I expect he's a bit fed up now. Nearly everyone is just when this winter spell of weather and work is over and before summer comes. Time has passed quite rapidly and will pass more quickly now I expect.

I have had a slight dose of influenza these last few days and now we are back resting have been sent by the MO for a rest to a convalescent home. I'm not at all bad so don't worry but after six months of worry with Brigade and with a new CO arriving ready to get everything spick and span I am pleased I haven't to work away again for a few days. Things will be in a pretty awful muddle with my being away I expect but Col Ussher will just have to kick his heels till I get back – then there'll be some clean up.

Rather unfortunate in every way that Col Smith is going away. I lose everything. We had got on good terms and he left things pretty much to me and backed me up but now this old boy won't know me and I expect rows so I ain't particularly happy.

Well I haven't much more to say. I hope everyone is quite well and getting on all right. I may get home on leave soon. Meantime things are excellent and I'm having a good rest. With love from DB Keith

31.3.16

My dear Mother,

I got your letter and parcels all right for which many thanks. I thought I had told you I got the Canisbay stuff some time ago and I wrote and thanked the secretary for the parcel. It was not, however, Miss Forbes. I also got some time ago an excellent cake from Helen Bruce for which I forgot to thank her which you might do for me on the first chance.

Jul has a lot of people looking after her and ought to get a good start off anyway. Has Will got any idea of what kind of a boat he will get posted to – a Cruiser or TBD [torpedo boat destroyer]? It ought to be exciting for him – if he is not seasick quite jolly as mostly they get lots of opportunity for leave and relaxation.

I am still resting but expect to rejoin the Regiment any day now and am not too sanguine as to how I shall get on with Col Ussher. Everyone is fed up that he has come back. With Col Smith I got on tremendously and we were the best regiment in the Brigade. Now we will be one of the best Regiments out here but most of us will be too much civilians to get on with a man who commanded a regular Battalion four years ago – when his time was up sent in an adverse report about his second in command and who when the 10th was formed got rid of about two majors, three captains and several other officers. However, if we don't get on I may get someone to get me a transfer into some-thing else. All that of course is in the air but I haven't learned to ride yet and I don't think Col Ussher will like an adjutant who can't ride.

I saw from the casualties that George's lot had suffered somewhat. We have not had so much, on the whole a quiet enough time but I expect now spring has come things will not stand still.

Leave is in prospect but not mine – it will be jolly nice when it arrives.

Well I'm ending up now as there is nothing much to say. We are back out of the line for quite a time now. With love to all from DB Keith.

11.4.16

My dear Mother,

It's a long time since I wrote you but I've been busy. Well first of all we're away back ever so far and not returning to the line for a few weeks yet. And it's a very nice country village we are in and the weather till today is excellent and we're all getting sunburnt.

Since I came out of hospital I've been on three days' manoeuvres which consisted mainly in galloping sometimes willingly and other times unwillingly across country and over ploughed fields. Happily I remained on the horse. I saw George just after I had got back to the regiment. I left him, however, rather hurriedly as the pony went off with its head down at a considerable gallop and I was more or less run away with for about three miles. However, we got home safely.

Leave at present is off. Some time soon it may probably reopen tho' it may be a month yet before I get home.

I must stop now but will write you later. Hope all are well. With love from DB Keith

Barrogill's letters end here. During 1917 he was hospitalised, and also received the Military Cross. By 1918 he was using his legal training and working in the Judge Advocate's Department. One final letter has survived from October 1918 – around the time Christina was arriving in Dieppe:

28.10.18

Headquarters, Vth Corps A, BEF

My dear Mother,

Not much has happened since I last wrote – still in the same place, peaceable as ever. It's rather an interesting place too – we've got a big Boche cemetery here and it could easily compare with any cemetery I've seen anywhere for arrangement, care and beauty. Everything is of course primitive but there's a lot of very good solid architecture about the place and two very fine monuments – not to anybody in particular – but just the cemetery. The whole thing is worked in a design with boxwood borders, massive crosses and green shrubs. There are several of our fellows buried here and their graves and crosses are excellently looked after. I've never seen any of our cemeteries to come within miles of it and it makes one rather ashamed of our yarns about Boche boiling down corpses for oil to see how well he has looked after the cemetery.

Stranger things happen in war than in fiction. When arriving through one of the villages near here our people got hold of a fellow officer whom the French women had hidden for four years since the Mons retreat. At first he was suspect so they hauled him up before the first Officer who came along who happened to be a cavalry officer and on looking at the fellow this officer recognised him as a trooper whom he last saw, within a mile of the village where he was found, away back in 1914 during the Retreat.

Well there's no news really – I've just been filling in some pages as I never do manage to write any stuff. Also I hear there's lots and lots of influenza about and hope nobody's got any – if anyone gets it I suppose it will be Tiny and if she does I hope she looks after herself and isn't silly about it 'cause there's a good deal of fatality this time isn't there.

I may put off my leave to Xmas as everybody will be home then but haven't quite decided yet. How is George – looking fit?

If possible could you send one brace grouse to Miss Rona Johnstone, 47 Ann Street Edinburgh – that's the wee kid Johnstone – Edith's sister. And if you have plenty if you sent two brace (cooked) to Major HOBBS, Staff Captain, ABBEVILLE AREA APOS I, I should be much obliged. He was awfully decent to me when I was there and there are eight or so of them in his Mess. If there's another brace to spare you might send one sometime to Captain PARKER Garrison Quartermaster, Headquarters CALAIS BASE where I was sometime ago. But there's no hurry.

Hope all are well, love to all, from DB Keith

Sources and further reading

Manuscript Collections

Keith Family Papers [P38], Highland Archive Service, Caithness Archive Centre
Papers of Albert Percy Braddock relating to the YMCA [YMCA/ACC15], Cadbury
    Research Library: Special Collections, University of Birmingham
Diaries of Professor John Wight Duff, Robinson Library Special Collections,
    Newcastle University [Duff Diaries]
Records of the Edinburgh Ladies' Education Association, University of Edinburgh
    Special Collections

Publications

Herbert Albert Laurens Fisher, *A Short Record of the Educational Work of the
    YMCA with the British Armies in France, with a foreword by the Rt Hon H.A.L.
    Fisher MP (President of the Board of Education)*, 1919
Sheila Hamilton, 'The First Generations of University Women', in Gordon
    Donaldson (ed.) *Four centuries: Edinburgh University Life*, 1983
Christina Keith, *The Romance of Barrogill Castle, the Queen Mother's New Home*, 1954

Christina Keith, *The Russet Coat: A critical study of Burns' poetry and of its background*, 1956

Christina Keith, *The Author of Waverley: a study in the personality of Sir Walter Scott*, 1964

David Barrogill Keith, *Book of the 12th Battalion Scottish Rifles*, 1920 (privately printed)

Allan C. Lannon, *Miller Academy History and Memories for the Millennium*, 2000

Dugald MacEchern, *The Sword of the North: Highland Memories of the Great War*, 1923

S. Manning, 'Women from Scotland at Newnham: the early years' in Mary Masson and Deborah Simonton (eds), *Women and Higher Education: Past, Present and Future*, 1996

Henrietta Munro, 'A Caithness School in the Early Nineteenth Century', in *Caithness Field Club Bulletin*, 1981

Ann Philips (ed.), *A Newnham Anthology*, 1973

Margaret Rayner, *The Centenary History of St Hilda's College, Oxford*, 1993

Alasdair Roberts, *Crème de la Crème: Girls' Schools of Edinburgh*, 2007

Annabel Robinson, *The Life and Work of Jane Ellen Harrison*, 2002

Jane Robinson, *Bluestockings: The remarkable story of the first women to fight for an education*, 2009

Michael Snape (ed.), *The Back Parts of War: The YMCA Memoirs and Letters of Barclay Baron*, 2009

Virginia Woolf, *A Room of One's Own*, 1929

Oxford Dictionary of National Biography

St Hilda's College Report and Supplement, 1962/3 (obituaries)

The Red Triangle and *The Red Triangle Bulletin*, periodicals of the YMCA

Index

Lightning Source UK Ltd.
Milton Keynes UK
UKOW05f2227140214

226515UK00004B/57/P